ONE WARS

WITHDRAWN

CHARACTER ENCYCLOPEDIA

JOIN THE BATTLE!

WRITTEN BY JASON FRY

CONTENTS

INTRODUCTION

For seven seasons and more than 130 episodes, *Star Wars: The Clone Wars* told the story of a war that ravaged the galaxy, pitting the Jedi Knights and the brave clones of the Grand Army of the Republic against billions of Separatist battle droids controlled by shadowy Sith villains.

That story gave us heroes to cheer, such as Anakin Skywalker, Captain Rex, and Ahsoka Tano. It gave us villains to fear, such as Darth Sidious, Count Dooku, and General Grievous. And it introduced us to characters caught in the middle and trying to survive, such as the charming pirate Hondo Ohnaka, the noble Duchess Satine Kryze, and the Nightsister Asajj Ventress.

We came to know not just these major characters, but hundreds of others—clone troopers, bounty hunters, pirates, politicians, droids, and ordinary citizens. Even those whose appearances were brief got a chance to shine thanks to Dave Filoni, George Lucas, and a team of talented writers, directors, and animators, with a single line of dialogue or a mere glimpse of an interesting costume suggesting rich lives filled with fascinating stories.

Star Wars: The Clone Wars: Character Encyclopedia Join the Battle! is an exploration of more than 350 of these characters, offering information about their homeworlds and abilities, backgrounds and fates. Entries in this book are organized according to the faction a character belongs to. The dating system used in the timelines indicates how many years before *Star Wars: A New Hope* an event occurs in the galaxy, denoted by BSW4.

This book is also a celebration of the show that introduced these characters to us and brought us thrilling new chapters in the ever-expanding saga of a galaxy far, far away....

YODA

JEDI GRANDMASTER

Yoda leads the Jedi Order, and has trained apprentices for centuries. With the Republic in danger, he agrees that the Jedi will become generals, leading the new clone army into battle. But he fears that abandoning their role as peacekeepers will cause the Jedi to lose their way and endanger the Order's future.

"IN THIS WAR, A DANGER THERE IS, OF LOSING WHO WE ARE."

– Yoda

CARING FOR THE CHOSEN ONE

Yoda reluctantly allowed Anakin Skywalker to train as a Jedi, agreeing he had enormous potential but fearing his emotional attachments made him vulnerable to the dark side of the Force. Anakin becomes a powerful Jedi, but Yoda remains concerned. During the Battle of Christophsis, he makes the surprising decision to assign Ahsoka Tano to Anakin as a Padawan, ignoring Skywalker's protests that a student will just slow him down. Yoda's hope is that learning to manage his relationship with Ahsoka will teach Anakin better control of his other, more dangerous emotions.

THE SHROUD OF THE DARK SIDE

Yoda values life, insisting that the Jedi treat the clones in their armies as individuals and not disposable soldiers born for war. But his worries grow as he learns it was the Sith who secretly created the clones and set the war in motion.

Short-bladed lightsaber is ideal for Yoda's fighting style

SPECIES: Unknown
HEIGHT: 0.66 m (2 ft 2 in)
ALLEGIANCE: Jedi Order
HOMEWORLD: Unknown

ABILITIES: Force sensitivity, leadership, lightsaber combat, teaching, diplomacy

The dark side shrouds Yoda's sense of the Force, but he begins to fear the war will not be won, and the Jedi will prove unable to escape the trap set by their Sith enemies.

THE DEAD SPEAK

In the last year of the war, Yoda hears the voice of Jedi Master Qui-Gon Jinn, who has somehow maintained his identity after death. Guided by Qui-Gon and accompanied by R2-D2, Yoda begins a quest that takes him to various locations across the galaxy. Through many tests and trials, Yoda gains surprising new knowledge of the Force. After the fall of the Jedi and the Republic, Yoda goes into exile on the planet of Dagobah. He learns to preserve his spirit as Qui-Gon has, meditating on the Force's mysteries.

TIMELINE

22 BSW4	Leads clone army at the First Battle of Geonosis
22 BSW4	Assigns Ahsoka Tano to Anakin as his Padawan
21 BSW4	Defends Coruscant from the Zillo Beast
20 BSW4	Agrees to fake Obi-Wan Kenobi's death to investigate assassination plot against Chancellor Palpatine
20 BSW4	Instructs younglings on sacred Jedi world of Ilum
19 BSW4	Hears voice of Qui-Gon Jinn and travels to Dagobah, where he experiences visions
19 BSW4	Passes the Five Priestesses' Force trials and is allowed to learn to preserve his identity after death
19 BSW4	Reluctantly agrees to target Count Dooku for assassination
19 BSW4	Assists Kashyyyk's Wookiee defenders against a Separatist invasion force
19 BSW4	Survives Order 66, but fails to defeat Darth Sidious and flees Coruscant
19 BSW4	Goes into exile on Dagobah

Simple, rough robe made of worn cloth

MACE WINDU

PROTECTOR OF THE REPUBLIC

Resolute and serious, Mace Windu is known for his lightsaber skills and his weapon's rare amethyst blade. Windu trusts few outside of the Jedi Order. He comes to view the Galactic Senate as weak and corrupt, damaged by Separatist plotters whose goal is to destroy both the Republic and the Jedi.

DEFENDER OF THE ORDER

Windu sees the Jedi as defenders of the galaxy's ordinary citizens against evildoers, a role he believes the Senate is too flawed to play. His highest loyalty is to the Jedi Order, and he will do anything to defend it against enemies, be they from the outside world or rebellious Jedi within its ranks. Windu has little tolerance for Jedi who disobey the Order's Council or question its masters, as Anakin Skywalker and Ahsoka Tano discover.

Windu can be a skilled diplomat when the situation requires it. He persuades Senator Orn Free Taa and the Twi'lek guerrilla leader Cham Syndulla to put aside their suspicions and work together to help the Republic retake the planet Ryloth. Windu then leads the assault on Ryloth's capital, Lessu, and personally captures Wat Tambor, the warlord who looted the planet during the Separatist occupation.

FACING A GROWING PERIL

As the Clone Wars intensify, Windu pushes the Jedi to take actions once considered unthinkable. He approves sending Jedi Master Quinlan Vos to eliminate Count Dooku and agrees the Order should keep silent about its discovery that the Sith created the clone army. In the wars' last days, he calls for the arrest of Supreme Chancellor Palpatine if he refuses to surrender his wartime powers, and taking over the Senate. This leads to an epic confrontation with Palpatine that the great Jedi will not survive.

SPECIES:	Human	ABILITIES:	Force sensitivity,

SPECIES: Human
HEIGHT: 1.88 m (6 ft 2 in)
ALLEGIANCE: Jedi Order
HOMEWORLD: Haruun Kal

ABILITIES: Force sensitivity, lightsaber combat, leadership, diplomacy, battle meditation, awareness of shatterpoints

Senses "shatterpoints," key moments where action can change events

TIMELINE

22 BSW4	Fights in the First Battle of Geonosis, killing bounty hunter Jango Fett
21 BSW4	Captures Separatist leader Wat Tambor on Ryloth
21 BSW4	Foils plot by bounty hunter Cad Bane to bomb Jedi Temple
21 BSW4	Stops Malastare's leader from killing the Zillo Beast
21 BSW4	Escapes assassination attempt by Jango's son Boba Fett
20 BSW4	Agrees to fake Obi-Wan Kenobi's death to investigate plot against Supreme Chancellor Palpatine
19 BSW4	Votes to expel Ahsoka Tano from the Order so she can face a Republic trial
19 BSW4	Foils Mother Talzin's plan to gain new Force powers
19 BSW4	Agrees to target Count Dooku for assassination
19 BSW4	Fights at Anaxes, ensuring Republic victory
19 BSW4	Dies trying to arrest Palpatine

Jedi boots offer excellent traction in combat

DISTINCTIVE SABER
Windu wields a lightsaber with a distinctive amethyst blade, electrum finish, and specially designed hilt.

"I SENSE A PLOT TO DESTROY THE JEDI."

– Mace Windu

ANAKIN SKYWALKER

THE CHOSEN ONE

Anakin Skywalker is the greatest hero of the Jedi Order. He is a bold commander in the Clone Wars, a peerless warrior with a lightsaber, and an amazing pilot. He has astonishing abilities with the Force, but also struggles with his emotions and with the secrets he keeps from the Jedi and his closest friends.

"YOU ARE THE CHOSEN ONE... BUT BEWARE YOUR HEART."

– The Father

AN ANCIENT PROPHECY

Jedi Master Qui-Gon Jinn considered Anakin the Chosen One of Jedi prophecy, fated to bring balance to the Force. But the Jedi disagree on what that prophecy means. Some fear Anakin's intense emotions and powers make him dangerous. In the strange Force realm of Mortis, Anakin experiences a chilling vision of the future, and what his destiny will mean for the galaxy. He is made to forget this horrifying sight by a powerful being known as The Father.

A SECRET MARRIAGE

Anakin's greatest secret is his marriage to Padmé Amidala, which, if discovered, would cause him to be thrown out of the Jedi Order. When his duties allow it, Anakin slips away from the Jedi Temple and the Clone Wars for a few precious hours with his wife. But Anakin's devotion to Padmé leaves him vulnerable to the anger and fear he struggles to control, and those are risky emotions for a Jedi.

The Force allows Anakin to see things before they happen

Mechanical hand replaces one cut off by Count Dooku

SPECIES: Human
HEIGHT: 1.85 m (6 ft 1 in)
ALLEGIANCE: Jedi Order
HOMEWORLD: Tatooine

ABILITIES: Exceptional Force sensitivity, expert pilot, superb mechanic, lightsaber combat

While Anakin is a good and loyal friend, such attachments are discouraged by the Jedi, for fear that they will cloud a Force user's judgment.

Yoda opposed training Anakin as a Jedi because of his attachment to his mother, who he had to leave behind on Tatooine, and has watched him with great concern during his years training under Obi-Wan. He assigns Ahsoka to become Anakin's Padawan in the hope that learning to part with a student will also teach Anakin to let go of other attachments. But master and Padawan soon form a powerful bond.

TIMELINE

41 BSW4	Born to Shmi Skywalker, without a father
32 BSW4	Discovered on Tatooine and becomes Obi-Wan Kenobi's Padawan
22 BSW4	Rescues Obi-Wan on Geonosis and loses his arm in a duel against Count Dooku
22 BSW4	Assigned Ahsoka Tano as a Padawan
20 BSW4	Brings balance to the Force on Mortis
19 BSW4	Clears Ahsoka of suspicion in Temple bombing
19 BSW4	Learns Dooku is the mysterious Darth Tyranus
19 BSW4	Rescues Palpatine from Grievous and kills Dooku
19 BSW4	Helps kill Mace Windu and becomes Sith Lord Darth Vader
19 BSW4	Leads assault on Jedi Temple as part of Order 66
19 BSW4	Strangles Padmé on Mustafar and duels Obi-Wan
19 BSW4	Rescued by Palpatine and encased in armor to preserve his life

ANAKIN'S ATTACHMENTS

Anakin is devoted to those he loves and often disregards Jedi orders and military procedures to rush off and help them. His circle of devotion includes his wife Padmé, his former master Obi-Wan Kenobi, Captain Rex, the loyal astromech R2-D2, and his Padawan Ahsoka Tano.

OBI-WAN KENOBI

JEDI NEGOTIATOR

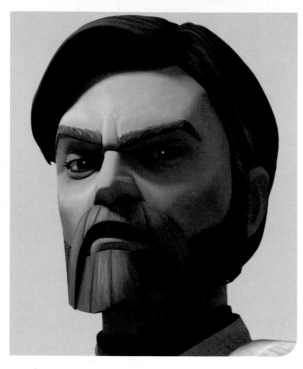

Obi-Wan Kenobi trained Anakin Skywalker, and master and former Padawan have become close friends. Though skilled with a lightsaber, Obi-Wan views war as a last resort, preferring to find a peaceful solution. He is one of the Jedi's most valuable negotiators, undertaking many diplomatic missions for the Republic.

AN IDEAL JEDI KNIGHT
Obi-Wan Kenobi has experience with difficult people: his own master, Qui-Gon Jinn, was a maverick who often quarreled with the Jedi Council, and Anakin was a reckless and disobedient Padawan. Obi-Wan makes his way through the galaxy with humor and patience, ready with a joke and a smile for Quinlan Vos, Captain Rex, Hondo Ohnaka, and the many others he meets on far-flung planets that become battlefields in the Clone Wars.

Obi-Wan finds particular amusement in watching Anakin struggle to teach his Padawan, Ahsoka Tano, who proves just as rash and difficult as Anakin was. Obi-Wan's former student is now learning the frustrations of being a teacher.

THE SHADOW OF THE PAST
When troubles arise on the neutral planet Mandalore, Obi-Wan's past catches up with him. As a Padawan, he and Duchess Satine Kryze fell in love, and Obi-Wan considered leaving the Jedi Order for her. When Maul kills Satine and seizes control of Mandalore, Obi-Wan struggles not to give in to sorrow and fury, knowing they can lead to the dark side.

SPECIES: Human
HEIGHT: 1.79 m (5 ft 10 in)
ALLEGIANCE: Jedi Order
HOMEWORLD: Stewjon

ABILITIES: Force sensitivity, lightsaber combat, leadership, teaching, diplomacy

Utility pouches on belt hold useful tools

Ready stance lets Jedi respond to foe's moves

TIMELINE

32 BSW4	Defeats Darth Maul, agrees to train Anakin Skywalker
22 BSW4	Discovers clone army on Kamino
22 BSW4	Rescued by Jedi and fights in the First Battle of Geonosis
19 BSW4	Discovers Count Dooku is Darth Tyranus and Sith created clone army
19 BSW4	Frees Palpatine after his kidnapping by Grievous
19 BSW4	Tracks Grievous to Utapau and destroys him, then narrowly survives Order 66
19 BSW4	Duels Darth Vader on Mustafar, leaving him apparently dead
19 BSW4	Goes into exile on Tatooine to watch over Anakin's newborn son, Luke

BORROWED PROTECTION

Early in the Clone Wars, many Jedi wear partial armor over their robes. This offers additional protection in chaotic battles and shows the clone troopers that their new Jedi generals are wartime comrades.

"IT TAKES STRENGTH TO RESIST THE DARK SIDE. ONLY THE WEAK EMBRACE IT."

– Obi-Wan Kenobi

AHSOKA TANO

A PADAWAN AT WAR

Ahsoka Tano is just 14 when she becomes Anakin Skywalker's Padawan. Brash at first, she matures quickly, bonding with Anakin and earning respect from the clones under her command. But she begins to doubt her place in the Jedi Order and leaves the Jedi path to pursue her own destiny.

WHEN "SNIPS" MET "SKYGUY"
Anakin and Ahsoka's relationship doesn't get off to a great start: he doesn't want a Padawan, particularly not one who is inexperienced and argues with him. But Anakin soon comes to respect Ahsoka's bravery and determination and recognizes she's just as reckless as he is. Over the next three years they become close and learn to depend on each other, with Anakin teaching Ahsoka the hard lessons of war.

A NEW PATH
As the Clone Wars draw to a close, Ahsoka's relationship with the Order is shattered by the actions of another Jedi. Ahsoka is accused of bombing the Jedi Temple and expelled from the Order to face a Republic military trial. Her friend Barriss Offee is quickly revealed as the real traitor, but Ahsoka turns down the offer to rejoin the Order, seeking a new life in Coruscant's underlevels. She falls in with the Martez sisters, who teach her the tough realities of life far from the Jedi Temple.

Ahsoka later agrees to help Bo-Katan Kryze's Nite Owl commandos retake their planet Mandalore from former Sith Lord Maul. She contacts Anakin and helps arrange a deal: the Republic will help Bo-Katan if she turns Maul over to them. Reunited with Rex and his clones,

SPECIES: Togruta
HEIGHT: 1.7 m (5 ft 7 in)
ALLEGIANCE: Jedi Order
HOMEWORLD: Shili

ABILITIES: Force sensitivity, lightsaber combat, exceptional agility, leadership, teaching, military tactics

Montrals grow as Togrutas mature

Ahsoka captures Maul but is nearly killed when the clones obey Order 66. She manages to remove Rex's inhibitor chip, and they escape to seek new lives away from the Empire.

Ahsoka favors reverse grip in lightsaber combat

TIMELINE

36 BSW4	Born on Shili
33 BSW4	Brought to Coruscant by Plo Koon to enter Jedi Order
22 BSW4	Assigned to Anakin Skywalker as his Padawan
20 BSW4	Dies on Mortis and is restored to life by the Daughter
19 BSW4	Framed for bombing of Jedi Temple and expelled from Order
19 BSW4	Cleared of involvement in bombing, but refuses to rejoin Jedi
19 B3W4	Recruited by Do-Katan Kryze to help free the planet Mandalore from Maul
19 BSW4	Captures Maul and transports him to Coruscant onboard the *Tribunal* until Order 66 diverts them
19 BSW4	Escapes Order 66 and flees into the Outer Rim

"I HAVE TO SORT THIS OUT ON MY OWN. WITHOUT THE COUNCIL, AND WITHOUT YOU."

– Ahsoka Tano

SHAAK TI

PROTECTOR OF CLONES

Patterns evolved to confuse predators on Shili

Outfit combines Jedi robes with Togruta dress

SPECIES: Togruta
HEIGHT: 1.87 m (6 ft 2 in)
ALLEGIANCE: Jedi Order
HOMEWORLD: Shili

ABILITIES: Force sensitivity, lightsaber combat, leadership, combat instruction, diplomacy

Jedi Council member Shaak Ti is sent to the planet Kamino at the start of the war to supervise the clone program. She proves sympathetic and caring, treating clone cadets like individuals instead of seeing them as organic products, as Kaminoan scientists do. Shaak Ti helps coordinate the planet's defenses when Separatist forces mount an invasion.

"UNITY WINS WAR, GENTLEMEN."

– Shaak Ti

A MALFUNCTIONING CLONE

The clone trooper Tup is sent to Kamino after killing his Jedi general, leading to the discovery of a tumor in his brain. Shaak Ti is puzzled when another clone, Fives, claims Tup's tumor is a malfunctioning inhibitor chip, similar to one in every clone's brain. The incident raises disturbing questions about the Kaminoans and the army they have created.

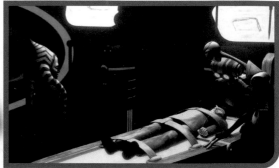

QUI-GON JINN

A VOICE FROM THE BEYOND

SPECIES: Human
HEIGHT: 1.93 m (6 ft 4 in)
ALLEGIANCE: Jedi Order
HOMEWORLD: Coruscant

ABILITIES: Force sensitivity, lightsaber combat, Jedi mysticism, teaching, diplomacy

Jedi Master Qui-Gon Jinn trained Obi-Wan Kenobi and discovered Anakin Skywalker, whom he believed was the Chosen One from Jedi prophecy. Qui-Gon died on Naboo but had learned to retain his identity after death through the Force. Years later, his spirit speaks to his old friends, revealing startling secrets about the Force.

THE WILL OF THE FORCE

Qui-Gon appears to Obi-Wan and Anakin on Mortis, warning of the dangers the strange realm poses to Anakin. Later, he summons Yoda to the planet Dagobah. Yoda passes a series of mystical tests and is allowed to learn how to preserve his own identity after death, with Qui-Gon as his teacher.

"I EXIST WHERE THERE IS NO FUTURE, OR PAST."

— Qui-Gon Jinn

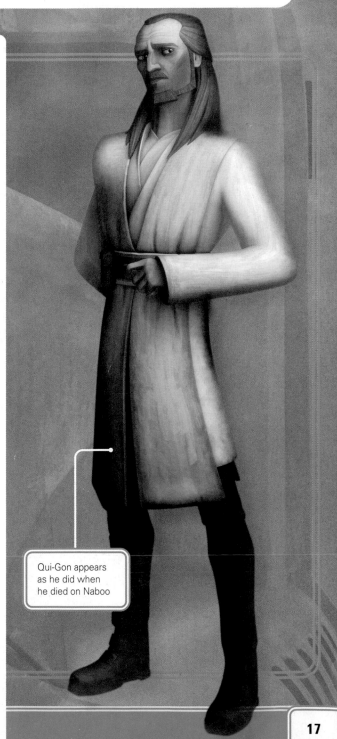

Qui-Gon appears as he did when he died on Naboo

BARRISS OFFEE

SPECIES: Mirialan
HEIGHT: 1.66 m (5 ft 5 in)
ALLEGIANCE: Jedi Order
HOMEWORLD: Mirial

ABILITIES: Force sensitivity, lightsaber combat, able to memorize complex patterns and data

Barriss Offee is Luminara Unduli's model student. She is a loyal, quiet Padawan who strikes up an unlikely friendship with the brash Ahsoka Tano on a challenging mission during the Second Battle of Geonosis.

But as the Clone Wars grind on, Barriss loses her faith in the Jedi, concluding that they are the true villains of the conflict. Barriss conspires with terrorist Letta Turmond to bomb the Jedi Temple and then frames Ahsoka for the crime. Brought to justice by Anakin Skywalker, Barriss defiantly admits her actions, accusing the Order of having abandoned its values.

LUMINARA UNDULI

Mirial chin tattoo symbolizes personal achievement

SPECIES: Mirialan
HEIGHT: 1.76 m (5 ft 9 in)
ALLEGIANCE: Jedi Order
HOMEWORLD: Mirial

ABILITIES: Force sensitivity, lightsaber combat, mind-probing, diplomacy, extreme physical flexibility

A respected Jedi Master known for her firm ways, Luminara Unduli believes Padawans should be well prepared for missions and not reckless. She sees her own apprentice, Barriss Offee, as the perfect example. Luminara's rigid views sometimes cause her to underestimate opponents.

Early in the war, Luminara and Ahsoka Tano transport criminal Nute Gunray to Coruscant. When Dooku's apprentice Asajj Ventress attacks, Luminara ignores Ahsoka's warnings about Ventress, doubting a wild and untrained Force-user can be a threat to her. Luminara soon learns she has made a costly mistake.

KIT FISTO

SPECIES: Nautolan
HEIGHT: 1.96 m (6 ft 5 in)
ALLEGIANCE: Jedi Order
HOMEWORLD: Glee Anselm

ABILITIES: Force sensitivity, lightsaber combat, acute senses, pheromone sensitivity, expert pilot

Jedi Master Kit Fisto can breathe in both air and water, and proves a fierce fighter in ground battles and in undersea combat. He is known among the Jedi for his easygoing ways and his ready smile, which he sometimes flashes in the midst of a grueling battle.

On the moon Vassek 3, Kit learns a hard lesson about the dangers the war poses to the Jedi. His former Padawan, Nahdar Vebb, discovers General Grievous' lair and is eager to capture him. Kit urges caution, but Nahdar ignores the warning, falling victim to the Separatist commander's lightsabers.

PLO KOON

SPECIES: Kel Dor
HEIGHT: 1.88 m (6 ft 2 in)
ALLEGIANCE: Jedi Order
HOMEWORLD: Dorin

ABILITIES: Force sensitivity, lightsaber combat, resistance in vacuum, expert pilot

Plo Koon is a stern Jedi with a firm sense of right and wrong. But he also cares deeply for the clone troopers in his squad, named the Wolfpack, risking his own life in battle to save theirs.

Near the end of the Clone Wars, the Jedi detect a distress signal from a moon of Oba Diah. Plo Koon and his troopers investigate and find a wrecked shuttle assigned to Sifo-Dyas—the long-dead Jedi Master who secretly ordered the creation of the clone army. Plo Koon's find leads to troubling questions about the clones and their purpose.

Mask protects Plo Koon from oxygen, which is poisonous to Kel Dors

AAYLA SECURA

SPECIES: Twi'lek
HEIGHT: 1.7 m (5 ft 7 in)
ALLEGIANCE: Jedi Order
HOMEWORLD: Ryloth

ABILITIES: Force sensitivity, exceptional agility, lightsaber combat, martial arts, meditation

Aayla Secura is an agile Jedi hailed as one of the Order's most skilled fighters. While marooned on the planet Maridun, she draws on her time as a Padawan to help Ahsoka Tano learn to control her emotions and overcome her attachment to her master. Aayla dies on Felucia, cut down by her troops during Order 66.

ADI GALLIA

Armor previously used by Coruscant Guard

SPECIES: Tholothian
HEIGHT: 1.74 m (5 ft 9 in)
ALLEGIANCE: Jedi Order
HOMEWORLD: Tholoth

ABILITIES: Force sensitivity, lightsaber combat, diplomacy, starfighter piloting

Jedi Council member Adi Gallia is aggressive when on the battlefield and appreciates Anakin Skywalker's quick, decisive actions as a warrior. The two team up to rescue Master Eeth Koth from General Grievous above the world Saleucami. Adi then helps Obi-Wan Kenobi track Maul and Savage Opress to the planet Florrum, but is killed by Savage.

EVEN PIELL

SPECIES: Lannik
HEIGHT: 1.22 m (4 ft)
ALLEGIANCE: Jedi Order
HOMEWORLD: Lannik

ABILITIES: Force sensitivity, leadership, meditation, lightsaber combat

Even Piell is a grim Jedi Master who serves on the Council and is a staunch defender of its traditions. He dies after being broken out of the Separatist prison known as the Citadel. Before his death, Piell passes partial coordinates of the secret hyperspace lane known as the Nexus Route to Ahsoka Tano.

KI-ADI-MUNDI

SPECIES: Cerean
HEIGHT: 1.98 m (6 ft 6 in)
ALLEGIANCE: Jedi Order
HOMEWORLD: Cerea

ABILITIES: Force sensitivity, exceptional agility, armed and unarmed combat, meditation, lightsaber combat

Ki-Adi-Mundi is a conservative member of the Jedi Council who struggles to believe that the galaxy could change as quickly as it does during the Republic's chaotic last years. He fights bravely in both Battles of Geonosis and dies on the planet Mygeeto during Order 66.

PONG KRELL

SPECIES: Besalisk
HEIGHT: 2.36 m (7 ft 9 in)
ALLEGIANCE: Jedi Order, Sith
HOMEWORLD: Ojom

ABILITIES: Force sensitivity, double-bladed lightsaber expert, tactical expertise

Pong Krell is one of the Jedi's most effective generals, though units under his command suffer disturbingly high casualty counts. He betrays the Republic during the Battle of Umbara, maneuvering clones into fighting each other, and is killed by Dogma.

QUINLAN VOS

SPECIES: Kiffar
HEIGHT: 1.91 m (6 ft 3 in)
ALLEGIANCE: Jedi Order
HOMEWORLD: Kiffu

ABILITIES: Force sensitivity, psychometry, expert tracker, lightsaber combat, exceptional agility

The brash Jedi Quinlan Vos has the rare Force ability of psychometry, which means he can touch objects imbued with the Force and access the memories of the people who handled them. Vos is ordered to assassinate Count Dooku, so becomes an ally of Asajj Ventress and learns dark-side powers from her. Ventress sacrifices herself to save his life, helping him return from darkness.

SAESEE TIIN

SPECIES: Iktotchi
HEIGHT: 1.93 m (6 ft 4 in)
ALLEGIANCE: Jedi Order
HOMEWORLD: Iktotch

ABILITIES: Force sensitivity, lightsaber combat, telepathy, leadership, starfighter piloting

Saesee Tiin is a Jedi Council member who chooses his words carefully, quietly listening to debates and reflecting on the Force's will. He is a skilled starfighter pilot as well as a deadly foe with a lightsaber. Tiin fights at Umbara and helps rescue a team of Jedi from the grim prison known as the Citadel.

TERA SINUBE

SPECIES: Cosian
HEIGHT: 1.83 m (6 ft)
ALLEGIANCE: Jedi Order
HOMEWORLD: Cosia

ABILITIES: Force sensitivity, lightsaber combat, Jedi lore, expert on Coruscant underworld, investigation

Tera Sinube is a wise Jedi Master with an unlikely interest in Coruscant's criminal underworld. Sinube's specialty proves very useful to Ahsoka Tano after a criminal steals her lightsaber. Sinube helps her track down the missing Jedi weapon. He also teaches Ahsoka a valuable lesson: it's far better to take your time and figure out the right plan than to move quickly and wind up taking the wrong approach.

EETH KOTH

SPECIES: Zabrak
HEIGHT: 1.87 m (6 ft 2 in)
ALLEGIANCE: Jedi Order
HOMEWORLD: Iridonia

ABILITIES: Force sensitivity, lightsaber combat, armed and unarmed combat, exceptional agility

Eeth Koth is a member of the Jedi Council who is renowned as one of its finest lightsaber duelists. He is captured by General Grievous at Saleucami, but manages to reveal his location to the Jedi by using secret hand signals and is soon rescued. Koth leaves both the Council and the Order late in the Clone Wars.

OPPO RANCISIS

SPECIES: Thisspiasian
HEIGHT (COILED): 1.38 m
(4 ft 6 in)
ALLEGIANCE: Jedi Order
HOMEWORLD: Thisspias

ABILITIES: Force sensitivity,
leadership, battle meditation,
military tactics, lightsaber
combat, unarmed combat

Oppo Rancisis is one of the oldest members of the
Jedi Council. He is respected for his quiet wisdom and
devotion to the Force. Oppo was born to royal parents
on his homeworld of Thisspias and joined the Jedi
Order as an infant. He was later offered the throne of
his planet but chose a life of service to the galaxy over
becoming a monarch. His snakelike tail serves as a
potent weapon if he is forced to defend himself.

JOCASTA NU

SPECIES: Human
HEIGHT: 1.69 m (5 ft 7 in)
ALLEGIANCE: Jedi Order
HOMEWORLD: Coruscant

ABILITIES: Force sensitivity,
lightsaber combat, knowledge
of Jedi lore

Jocasta Nu is the chief librarian of the fabled
Jedi Archives. She is proud of the Order's
accumulated knowledge and impatient with
anyone bold enough to suggest there are
questions that the Archives can't answer.
Many Jedi still wince at the memory of a
stern lecture they received from Madame Nu
during their Padawan days.

PROFESSOR HUYANG

MODEL: Mark IV
architect droid
HEIGHT: 1.8 m (5 ft 11 in)
ALLEGIANCE: Jedi Order
MANUFACTURER: Unknown

ABILITIES: Jedi lore,
lightsaber construction,
teaching

Professor Huyang is an ancient droid
who has supervised lightsaber
construction for centuries,
teaching many younglings
the art of building their
first Jedi weapons.
He is based on
the *Crucible*, a
training vessel
rumored to be
as old as the
droid teacher
who calls
it home.

SIFO-DYAS

SPECIES: Human
HEIGHT: 1.8 m (5 ft 11 in)
ALLEGIANCE: Jedi Order
HOMEWORLD: Minashee

ABILITIES: Force sensitivity, lightsaber combat, knowledge of Jedi lore, foreknowledge and prophecy

Sifo-Dyas served on the Jedi Council in the years before the invasion of Naboo. He believed the Republic needed stronger defenses and secretly arranged for the Kaminoans to create a clone army. The Sith paid the Pykes, a criminal syndicate, to murder Sifo-Dyas and used the army against the Jedi.

IMA-GUN DI

SPECIES: Nikto
HEIGHT: 1.92 m (6 ft 4 in)
ALLEGIANCE: Jedi Order
HOMEWORLD: Kintan

ABILITIES: Force sensitivity, lightsaber combat, leadership, military tactics

Ima-Gun Di plays a key role in defending Ryloth against Separatist invasion, working with the guerrilla leader Cham Syndulla. Cut off and in danger of being overrun by battle droids, the Jedi sacrifices his life so Syndulla's Twi'leks can escape and continue the fight.

BOLLA ROPAL

SPECIES: Rodian
HEIGHT: 1.75 m (5 ft 9 in)
ALLEGIANCE: Jedi Order
HOMEWORLD: Rodia

ABILITIES: Force sensitivity, lightsaber combat, leadership, Jedi lore

Bolla Ropal is the guardian of a kyber memory crystal, which must be used in tandem with a holocron to reveal a record of Force-sensitive children across the galaxy. Cad Bane steals the crystal on behalf of the Sith, then tortures Ropal to make him unlock a holocron so the names can be read. Ropal resists and dies in the process.

COLEMAN KCAJ

SPECIES: Ongree
HEIGHT: 2.04 m (6 ft 8 in)
ALLEGIANCE: Jedi Order
HOMEWORLD: Skustell

ABILITIES: Force sensitivity, lightsaber combat, meditation, military strategy, diplomacy

The hulking Jedi Master Coleman Kcaj serves on the Jedi Council during the Clone Wars. Kcaj was a formidable warrior during his younger years but has come to see battles as tragic failures to find mutual understanding.

TIPLAR

SPECIES: Mikkian
HEIGHT: 1.8 m (5 ft 11 in)
ALLEGIANCE: Jedi Order
HOMEWORLD: Mikkia

ABILITIES: Force sensitivity, lightsaber combat, armed and unarmed combat, leadership, military tactics

The Mikkian Jedi Tiplar serves as a Jedi General during the Clone Wars, often fighting alongside her twin sister Tiplee. During the Battle of Ringo Vinda, the clone trooper Tup's inhibitor chip malfunctions, and he blasts Tiplar—killing her instantly.

TIPLEE

SPECIES: Mikkian
HEIGHT: 1.79 m (5 ft 10 in)
ALLEGIANCE: Jedi Order
HOMEWORLD: Mikkia

ABILITIES: Force sensitivity, lightsaber combat, armed and unarmed combat, leadership, military tactics

Jedi Tiplee fights alongside her twin sister and fellow Jedi Tiplar at Ringo Vinda. Tiplee helps organize a retreat after a clone kills Tiplar. Shortly afterward, Tiplee falls in combat against Count Dooku during a fight at a Mandalorian supply outpost on an asteroid.

RIG NEMA

SPECIES: Halaisi
HEIGHT: 1.8 m (5 ft 11 in)
ALLEGIANCE: Jedi Order
HOMEWORLD: Halais

ABILITIES: Force sensitivity, medicine, Jedi healing lore, meditation

Rig Nema serves the Jedi as a physician, with her specialties including physical health, mental well-being, and spiritual balance. When Yoda begins hearing voices, Dr. Nema suggests a risky and rarely used procedure designed to force Yoda into deep meditation, opening his consciousness.

KY NAREC

SPECIES: Human
HEIGHT: 1.92 m (6 ft 4 in)
ALLEGIANCE: Jedi Order
HOMEWORLD: Cosmatanic Steppes

ABILITIES: Force sensitivity, lightsaber combat, armed and unarmed combat, leadership, diplomacy

The Jedi Knight Ky Narec was marooned on the wild frontier planet Rattatak, where he saved a young Dathomirian exile, Asajj Ventress, from Weequay raiders and trained her in the ways of the Force. Narec's death leaves Asajj vulnerable to the dark side.

GUNGI

SPECIES: Wookiee
HEIGHT: 1.53 m (5 ft)
ALLEGIANCE: Jedi Order
HOMEWORLD: Kashyyyk

ABILITIES: Force sensitivity, lightsaber combat

Gungi is one of the few Wookiees in the Jedi Order. Gungi takes part in the Gathering alongside the rest of his youngling clan, journeying to Ilum to find a kyber crystal to power his lightsaber. Gungi is impulsive and aggressive, flaws he must overcome to reach his full potential as a member of the Jedi Order.

KATOONI

SPECIES: Tholothian
HEIGHT: 1.3 m (4 ft 3 in)
ALLEGIANCE: Jedi Order
HOMEWORLD: Tholoth

ABILITIES: Force sensitivity, lightsaber combat, strong leadership

Katooni is a Force-sensitive youngling, learning the ways of the Force on Coruscant, and helping the other members of her clan in the ritual known as the Gathering. The young Tholothian is a natural leader but must learn to trust in her growing skills and her sense of the Force. These abilities prove crucial in dealing with pirates and Separatists.

PETRO

SPECIES: Human
HEIGHT: 1.26 m (4 ft 2 in)
ALLEGIANCE: Jedi Order
HOMEWORLD: Corellia

ABILITIES: Force sensitivity, lightsaber combat

Petro dreams of proving himself as a great Jedi warrior, and his competitive streak often annoys his fellow younglings in his clan. After claiming his kyber crystal, Petro speedily builds his lightsaber but assembles it incorrectly, causing Professor Huyang to lecture him about the importance of following directions during Jedi traditions.

ZATT

SPECIES: Nautolan
HEIGHT: 1.21 m (4 ft)
ALLEGIANCE: Jedi Order
HOMEWORLD: Glee Anselm

ABILITIES: Force sensitivity, lightsaber combat

Zatt is a brainy Nautolan youngling who undergoes the rite of passage of the Gathering on Ilum as part of his Jedi training. Zatt loves tinkering with technology but must learn that science can't answer all of his problems. Sometimes a Jedi must also rely on faith in the Force and let it guide one's actions.

GANODI

SPECIES: Rodian
HEIGHT: 1.19 m (3 ft 11 in)
ALLEGIANCE: Jedi Order

HOMEWORLD: Rodia
ABILITIES: Force sensitivity, lightsaber combat

Ganodi is a member of a clan of younglings learning the ways of the Force in Coruscant's Jedi Temple. The promising student struggles with her own doubts. In Ilum's fabled Crystal Cave, Ganodi finds herself surrounded by kyber crystals. She must quiet her mind and let the Force tell her which of the hundreds of crystals is meant for her.

BYPH

SPECIES: Ithorian
HEIGHT: 1.22 m (4 ft)
ALLEGIANCE: Jedi Order

HOMEWORLD: Ithor
ABILITIES: Force sensitivity, lightsaber combat

Byph is a member of a clan who travels to Ilum for the Jedi trial known as the Gathering. His greatest challenge is to overcome his own fears, which often make situations seem worse than they actually are. Byph passes this test and later proves his worth against General Grievous' droid troops.

NAHDAR VEBB

SPECIES: Mon Calamari
HEIGHT: 1.86 m (6 ft 1 in)
ALLEGIANCE: Jedi Order
HOMEWORLD: Mon Cala

ABILITIES: Force sensitivity, lightsaber combat,

Nahdar Vebb learns from Kit Fisto as a Padawan, but the Clone Wars separate them and Nahdar passes the Jedi trials alone. Nahdar struggles to master his anger at the Separatists and falls in battle after confronting General Grievous.

JINX

SPECIES: Twi'lek
HEIGHT: 1.76 m (5 ft 9 in)
ALLEGIANCE: Jedi Order
HOMEWORLD: Ryloth

ABILITIES: Force sensitivity, unarmed combat, survival

Jinx's training as a youngling takes a grim turn when he and his friends are kidnapped and taken to the moon Wasskah to be hunted by Trandoshans. Jinx survives, but his normal optimism is sorely tested by this ordeal. He struggles to maintain his faith in his Jedi training and his trust in the Force.

KALIFA

SPECIES: Human
HEIGHT: 1.72 m (5 ft 8 in)
ALLEGIANCE: Jedi Order
HOMEWORLD: Corellia

ABILITIES: Force sensitivity, unarmed combat, strong leadership, survival

Kalifa emerges as the leader of the younglings trapped on Wasskah, doing her best to keep them from losing hope, while struggling with her own fear and anger. Ahsoka Tano gives her a new sense of hope, but Kalifa dies before she can escape the moon.

O-MER

SPECIES: Cerean
HEIGHT: 1.74 m (5 ft 9 in)
ALLEGIANCE: Jedi Order
HOMEWORLD: Cerea

ABILITIES: Force sensitivity, unarmed combat, agility, survival

O-Mer struggles to keep his faith while hunted by Trandoshans on the moon Wasskah. With Ahsoka Tano's help, he overcomes his fears and helps the younglings turn the tables on their tormenters, escaping the hunters' moon and returning to the Jedi.

DEPA BILLABA

SPECIES: Human
HEIGHT: 1.68 m (5 ft 6 in)
ALLEGIANCE: Jedi Order
HOMEWORLD: Chalacta

ABILITIES: Force sensitivity, lightsaber combat, starfighter piloting, armed and unarmed combat

Jedi Council member Depa Billaba was trained by Mace Windu. Depa and her young Padawan, Caleb Dume, are battling Separatists on Kaller when Order 66 turns their clone troopers against them. She sacrifices her life to let Caleb escape.

CALEB DUME

SPECIES: Human
HEIGHT: 1.4 m (4 ft 7 in)
ALLEGIANCE: Jedi Order
HOMEWORLD: Unknown

ABILITIES: Force sensitivity, lightsaber combat, armed and unarmed combat, military tactics

Caleb Dume studies under Jedi Master Depa Billaba and has a precocious interest in strategy and tactics. He flees Order 66 when Depa gives her life to save his. He is then left to survive as a fugitive under the new Galactic Empire.

CIN DRALLIG

SPECIES: Human
HEIGHT: 1.74 m (5 ft 9 in)
ALLEGIANCE: Jedi Order
HOMEWORLD: Lavisar

ABILITIES: Force sensitivity, lightsaber combat, armed and unarmed combat, teaching, leadership, knowledge of security

Cin Drallig supervises the Jedi Temple guard and is responsible for the Order's security on Coruscant. He is often called the Order's finest duelist and has taught many younglings to fight with a lightsaber. Drallig dies defending the Temple during the chaos of Order 66.

JEDI TEMPLE GUARD

SPECIES: Varies
HEIGHT: Varies
ALLEGIANCE: Jedi Order
HOMEWORLD: Varies

ABILITIES: Force sensitivity, lightsaber combat, armed and unarmed combat, military and security tactics

The Jedi Temple guard provides security for the Order's Temple on Coruscant, wielding double-bladed lightsaber pikes. Jedi Knights who join the guard surrender their identities to serve the Order. Their identical masks serve as symbols of this service and their emotional detachment.

PADMÉ AMIDALA

SENATOR WITH A SECRET

Padmé looks forward to her stolen moments with Anakin, but her duties as a senator and his responsibilities as a Jedi give them little time to be together. She develops a bond with Ahsoka Tano and Obi-Wan Kenobi, but because her marriage must be kept secret, she says little about the frightening moments when her husband is overcome by fear or fury.

Once Naboo's queen, Padmé Amidala now serves her homeworld as senator. While she supports Supreme Chancellor Palpatine, she worries that the war is damaging the Republic and hopes to find a peaceful solution. Padmé must outmaneuver her many enemies while preserving the secret that she is married to Jedi Anakin Skywalker.

AGGRESSIVE NEGOTIATOR

Padmé seeks peace and looks for the good in people, but she isn't naive. She remembers how Naboo suffered under occupation by the Trade Federation. Her first instinct is to solve problems through diplomacy, but should that fail, Padmé is skilled with a blaster and in unarmed combat. She needs these skills during the Clone Wars.

LOYAL TO THE REPUBLIC

Padmé supports Palpatine, having helped him become Supreme Chancellor during the Naboo crisis. But she becomes concerned about his growing powers, huge boosts to military spending, and the Republic's increasing control of the banks. Padmé finds allies in fellow senators Bail Organa and Mon Mothma, who encourage her to speak up in the Senate and become a powerful voice for the galaxy's ordinary citizens. Padmé barely outlives the Republic she loves and fights so hard to preserve, but the memory of her inspires her old friends Organa and Mothma to build a rebellion against Palpatine's Empire.

SPECIES: Human
HEIGHT: 1.65 m (5 ft 5 in)
ALLEGIANCE: Republic
HOMEWORLD: Naboo

ABILITIES: Diplomacy, leadership, public speaking

ELG-3A pistol is small but packs impressive punch

Battle dress offers mobility in combat

"IF WE CONTINUE TO IMPOVERISH OUR PEOPLE, IT IS NOT ON THE BATTLEFIELD WHERE DOOKU WILL DEFEAT US, BUT IN OUR OWN HOMES."

– Padmé Amidala

TIMELINE

46 BSW4	Born on Naboo
32 BSW4	Elected queen of Naboo
32 BSW4	Escapes Trade Federation invasion of Naboo and asks Senate for aid
32 BSW4	Introduces no-confidence vote in Chancellor Valorum, leading to Palpatine becoming Chancellor
28 BSW4	Becomes Naboo's senator
22 BSW4	Secretly marries Anakin Skywalker on Naboo
21 BSW4	Holds peace talks with Separatists on Raxus
21 D3W4	Gives well-received speech to Senate warning of costs of war to citizens
19 BSW4	Meets with other senators to discuss possible resistance to Palpatine's rule
19 BSW4	Dies giving birth to twins Luke and Leia

R2-D2

ADVENTUROUS ASTROMECH

Primary sensor eye

Power recharge coupling

MODEL: R-series astromech droid
HEIGHT: 0.96 m (3 ft 2 in)
ALLEGIANCE: Republic
MANUFACTURER: Industrial Automaton

ABILITIES: Starfighter piloting and maintenance, database for general repairs, information access and retrieval

R2-D2 serves Anakin Skywalker as his mechanic and piloting assistant, and has saved his impulsive master from many dangers. He is spunky, loyal, and stubborn, often to the annoyance of his good friend C-3PO. R2's circuits hold classified data, but Anakin refuses to erase his memory, seeing the droid's quirks as part of his personality.

A LITTLE SHORT FOR A COMBAT MODEL

R2-D2 is designed for repairing machinery and not for combat, but that doesn't stop him from wading into fights with Separatist astromechs or even super battle droids. He uses tools ranging from his electro-shock prod to his oil supply and rocket boosters to distract and defeat his opponents.

C-3PO

MASTER OF PROTOCOL

MODEL: 3PO-series protocol droid
HEIGHT: 1.73 m (5 ft 8 in)
ALLEGIANCE: Republic
MANUFACTURER: Custom-built
ABILITIES: Diplomacy, languages, knowledge of cultures and traditions

C-3PO is a golden droid programmed for etiquette and protocol, and fluent in more than six million forms of communication. He serves Padmé Amidala, but his mistress gets in a remarkable amount of trouble for a senator, forcing C-3PO to deal with many unpleasant and even dangerous situations.

> "ARTOO, BE QUIET. THIS SITUATION CALLS FOR MY MOST DELICATE DIPLOMATIC SKILLS."
>
> – C-3PO

UNLIKELY PARTNERSHIP
C-3PO was built by Anakin Skywalker from scavenged parts and later given to Padmé as a wedding gift. He often travels with R2-D2, whom C-3PO considers a good friend—despite R2's frustrating habit of being brave when any sensible droid would know to stay out of trouble.

Midsection lined with powerbus cables

Gold plating suitable for a diplomat

BAIL ORGANA

ELOQUENT POLITICIAN

Robes of wool crafted on Alderaan

SPECIES: Human
HEIGHT: 1.67 m (5 ft 6 in)
ALLEGIANCE: Republic
HOMEWORLD: Alderaan

ABILITIES: Diplomacy, leadership, knowledge of laws and traditions, public speaking

Bail Organa represents Alderaan in the Galactic Senate and is known for both his eloquent speeches and his skill in debates. He supports Supreme Chancellor Palpatine. However, he increasingly worries that the war is damaging the Republic and the foundations of its democracy.

"HE CARRIES A GREAT WEIGHT.
HE'S SEEN AS A VOICE OF REASON."

– Padmé Amidala

GATHERING ALLIES

Bail is skilled at building alliances and works closely with senators such as Mon Mothma, Onaconda Farr, and Padmé Amidala—who he encourages to become a passionate advocate for peace. He also reaches out to the Jedi Order, befriending Obi-Wan Kenobi and Yoda.

MON MOTHMA

CONSCIENCE OF THE REPUBLIC

SPECIES: Human
HEIGHT: 1.83 m (6 ft)
ALLEGIANCE: Republic
HOMEWORLD: Chandrila

ABILITIES: Diplomacy, leadership, Senate knowledge

Senator Mon Mothma of Chandrila is one of the most determined voices for peace and is respected throughout the Republic. She is a close ally of Bail Organa's and becomes a friend and mentor of Padmé Amidala, who she believes is one of the best hopes for preserving the Republic.

WAR BY ANOTHER NAME

Mothma and her Senate allies speak out against military spending, leading to disagreements with pro-military senators led by Kamino's Halle Burtoni. As the Clone Wars drag on, Mothma begins to fear that powerful forces within the Republic are as much a threat to it as the Separatist droid armies.

"WE ARE LOYALISTS, TRYING TO PRESERVE DEMOCRACY IN THE REPUBLIC."

– Mon Mothma

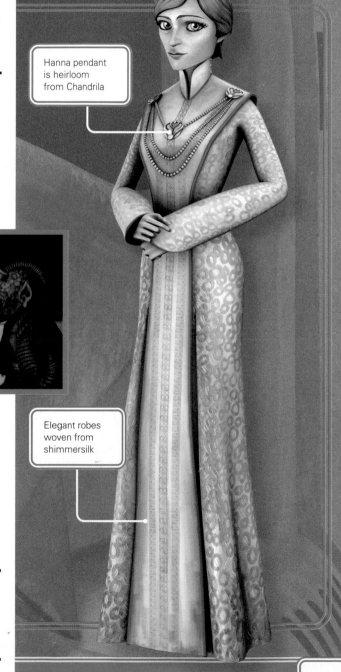

Hanna pendant is heirloom from Chandrila

Elegant robes woven from shimmersilk

ORN FREE TAA

SPECIES: Twi'lek
HEIGHT: 1.84 m (6 ft)
ALLEGIANCE: Republic
HOMEWORLD: Ryloth

ABILITIES: Political skills, diplomacy, leadership

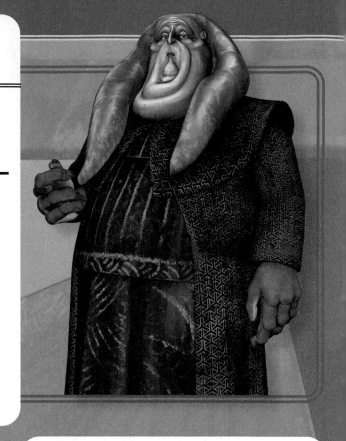

Orn Free Taa represents everything wrong with the Republic: he is corrupt, greedy, and more interested in power than in improving the lives of the Twi'leks he represents as Ryloth's senator. But he is a key Loyalist and an ally of Supreme Chancellor Palpatine, who is willing to overlook his many flaws.

When the Separatists invade Ryloth, Mace Windu encourages Taa and the guerrilla leader Cham Syndulla to put aside their differences to help the Republic's forces. Taa agrees that Republic troops will leave Ryloth after its liberation, and Syndulla agrees not to seek political office.

ONACONDA FARR

SPECIES: Rodian
HEIGHT: 1.75 m (5 ft 9 in)
ALLEGIANCE: Republic
HOMEWORLD: Rodia

ABILITIES: Diplomacy, legislative strategy, dealmaking

Senator Onaconda Farr of Rodia is an old friend of Padmé Amidala who advised her during her early days in the Senate. With the people of Rodia facing starvation, Farr agrees to hand Padmé over to the Separatists in return for relief supplies. This betrayal haunts Farr, though Padmé forgives her "Uncle Ono."

But others won't let go of the past. Farr works with Padmé and her Loyalist allies to seek peace despite being targeted by thugs and bounty hunters, but he dies after ingesting poison. An investigation reveals the killer is Lolo Purs, Rodia's Senate representative and Farr's supposedly loyal aide.

Gaudy robe made of Ottegan silk

JAR JAR BINKS

SPECIES: Gungan
HEIGHT: 1.96 m (6 ft 5 in)
ALLEGIANCE: Republic
HOMEWORLD: Naboo

ABILITIES: Hard to describe

Reluctantly taking up armaments

MAS AMEDDA

SPECIES: Chagrian
HEIGHT: 1.96 m (6 ft 5 in)
ALLEGIANCE: Republic
HOMEWORLD: Champala

ABILITIES: Bureaucracy, diplomacy, political skills

Mas Amedda is Vice Chairman of the Senate. He presides over the chamber during debates and works behind the scenes to make sure Supreme Chancellor Palpatine's programs are approved—a task to which he brings his skills at making deals, calling in favors, and pressuring reluctant politicians.

Amedda's bullying ways allow Palpatine to look reasonable and kindly, which works to the Chancellor's advantage. The Chagrian is one of the few beings in the galaxy to know Palpatine is actually Darth Sidious. Amedda survives the Clone Wars to serve as Grand Vizier of the Galactic Empire.

Jar Jar Binks is Naboo's accident prone Senate representative. He seems to attract trouble and misfortune, but somehow comes through it undamaged, except for his pride. His friends find him exasperating, but his kind heart and loyalty inspire them to overlook his many missteps and pratfalls.

While no warrior, Jar Jar will fight for his friends and for causes he holds dear. On Rodia, he saves Padmé from being taken captive by the vengeful Nute Gunray.

CAPTAIN ACKBAR

Battle baton can be used as a blaster

SPECIES: Mon Calamari
HEIGHT: 1.8 m (5 ft 11 in)
ALLEGIANCE: Mon Cala
HOMEWORLD: Mon Cala

ABILITIES: Military tactics, leadership, armed and unarmed combat

Gial Ackbar serves Prince Lee-Char of Mon Cala as captain of the Mon Calamari Guard and as his chief military advisor. He protects the prince when the Separatists try to overthrow him during Mon Cala's civil war, fighting alongside Mon Calamari, Jedi, Gungans, Quarren, and clone troopers.

PRINCE LEE-CHAR

SPECIES: Mon Calamari
HEIGHT: 1.7 m (5 ft 7 in)
ALLEGIANCE: Mon Cala
HOMEWORLD: Mon Cala

ABILITIES: Leadership, armed and unarmed combat

Mon Cala's young prince is forced to grow up fast when his father, King Kolina, is murdered, and Separatists goad Mon Cala's Quarren into battling their Mon Calamari neighbors, ending generations of peace. With the help of Captain Ackbar, Prince Lee-Char proves brave in battle and leads his people to victory over Riff Tamson and his armies. He then takes the throne and seeks to heal the divisions between the people on his planet.

Shell used to signal troops should advance

MEENA TILLS

SPECIES: Mon Calamari
HEIGHT: 1.71 m (5 ft 7 in)
ALLEGIANCE: Republic
HOMEWORLD: Mon Cala

ABILITIES: Leadership, diplomacy, knowledge of bureaucracy

Meena Tills represents Mon Cala in the Republic Senate. She hurries back to her homeworld with Padmé Amidala to offer help after the king's death causes a split between the planet's Quarren and Mon Calamari inhabitants. Tills is caught up in a civil war as Separatist droid armies, led by Riff Tamson, battle Prince Lee-Char and loyal Mon Calamari. She returns to Coruscant after Lee-Char's victory over Tamson's forces.

SIONVER BOLL

SPECIES: Bivall
HEIGHT: 1.73 m (5 ft 8 in)
ALLEGIANCE: Republic
HOMEWORLD: Protobranch

ABILITIES: Scientific knowledge, military research, engineering

Sionver Boll is a brilliant Republic scientist whose lab produces inventions useful in the war. Her prototype electro-proton bomb proves effective against droids on the planet Malastare but also frees a huge Zillo Beast from its lair beneath the ground. Boll studies the beast's scales, which could be useful in creating new clone armor, but objects to Palpatine's suggestion that she kill the creature.

CHEWBACCA

SPECIES: Wookiee
HEIGHT: 2.28 m (7 ft 6 in)
ALLEGIANCE: Wookiees
HOMEWORLD: Kashyyyk

ABILITIES: Starship piloting, armed and unarmed combat, agility, mechanical repairs, survival, strong leadership

Chewbacca is captured by Trandoshans and taken to the moon Wasskah to be hunted, but teams up with Ahsoka Tano to defeat the hunters. The capable warrior, mechanic, and pilot then returns to his homeworld, Kashyyyk, where he battles Separatists and assists Yoda in one of the Clone Wars' final battles.

TARFFUL

SPECIES: Wookiee
HEIGHT: 2.32 m (7 ft 7 in)
ALLEGIANCE: Wookiees
HOMEWORLD: Kashyyyk

ABILITIES: Armed and unarmed combat, military tactics, leadership

Brawny and powerful, Tarfful serves as a chieftain and general on Kashyyyk. He leads a rescue team to free Chewbacca from the moon Wasskah, where he delights in overpowering Trandoshan hunters who enjoy hunting helpless beings for sport. Tarfful fights alongside Yoda and Republic troops during the Battle of Kashyyyk.

BARON PAPANOIDA

SPECIES: Pantoran
HEIGHT: 1.77 m (5 ft 10 in)
ALLEGIANCE: Republic
HOMEWORLD: Pantora

ABILITIES: Politics, leadership, diplomacy, starship piloting, armed combat, investigation

Baron Papanoida is an influential political figure. He refuses to join the Separatists, so they blockade Pantora and hire a bounty hunter to kidnap his daughters. Unwilling to wait for Senate action, Papanoida investigates the crime himself, traveling to Tatooine to save his children from the galactic underworld.

CHI EEKWAY PAPANOIDA

SPECIES: Pantoran
HEIGHT: 1.65 m (5 ft 5 in)
ALLEGIANCE: Republic
HOMEWORLD: Pantora

ABILITIES: Legislative knowledge, diplomacy

Chi Eekway Papanoida is one of Baron Papanoida's daughters. When her father refuses to cooperate with the Separatists, the bounty hunter Greedo abducts her and her sister, Che Amanwe. Chi is held on a Trade Federation Droid Control Ship until she is rescued by Ahsoka Tano and Riyo Chuchi. She later succeeds Chuchi as Pantora's senator.

CHAIRMAN CHI CHO

Military cap with warm earmuffs

SPECIES: Pantoran
HEIGHT: 1.98 m (6 ft 6 in)
ALLEGIANCE: Republic
HOMEWORLD: Pantora

ABILITIES: Legislative knowledge, leadership

Chi Cho is chairman of Pantora and a fierce defender of his planet's interests. When Cho discovers white-furred Talz living on the icy world Orto Plutonia, which he sees as Pantoran property, he demands they submit or die. Cho's refusal to negotiate leads to his death, and Baron Papanoida succeeds him as chairman.

RIYO CHUCHI

SPECIES: Pantoran
HEIGHT: 1.65 m (5 ft 5 in)
ALLEGIANCE: Republic
HOMEWORLD: Pantora

ABILITIES: Leadership, diplomacy, political knowledge, investigation

Traditional golden Pantoran headdress

Riyo Chuchi is Pantora's young senator. She fails to convince Chairman Cho to seek a peaceful solution with the Talz they find living on Orto Plutonia. After Cho dies in a skirmish with the Talz, Chuchi wisely negotiates an end to hostilities. She later helps free Chi Eekway Papanoida from captivity.

LOLO PURS

SPECIES: Rodian
HEIGHT: 1.75 m (5 ft 9 in)
ALLEGIANCE: Republic
HOMEWORLD: Rodia

ABILITIES: Legislative strategy, political knowledge

Lolo Purs is Rodia's senate representative, assisting Senator Onaconda Farr. After Farr agrees to hand over Padmé Amidala to Trade Federation leader Nute Gunray, Purs concludes Farr has damaged their planet's honor and can no longer be senator. She poisons her mentor, but Padmé figures out who killed Farr. Purs admits her crime and is hauled off to jail.

LOTT DOD

SPECIES: Neimoidian
HEIGHT: 1.9 m (6 ft 3 in)
ALLEGIANCE: Republic (officially)

HOMEWORLD: Cato Neimoidia
ABILITIES: Influence-peddling, strategy, political knowledge, bureaucracy, manipulation

Miter indicates senatorial rank and status

Lott Dod represents the Trade Federation in the Republic Senate, though his Separatist affiliation is no secret. Dod gleefully uses his knowledge of Senate rules to protect other Separatist allies serving alongside him.

EDCEL BAR GANE

SPECIES: Roonan
HEIGHT: 1.72 m (5 ft 8 in)
ALLEGIANCE: Republic
HOMEWORLD: Roona

ABILITIES: Politics, legislative knowledge

Edcel Bar Gane is a veteran senator, who helped oust Supreme Chancellor Valorum years before the Clone Wars, and is an outspoken supporter of Palpatine. Bar Gane is hot-tempered and opposes any attempt to seek peace with the Separatists.

DOGE NAKHA URUS

SPECIES: Dug
HEIGHT: 1.12 m (3 ft 8 in)
ALLEGIANCE: Malastare
HOMEWORLD: Malastare

ABILITIES: Leadership, intimidation

Doge Nakha Urus drives a hard bargain when the Republic seeks access to his world's fuel reserves. He clashes with Mace Windu over the fate of a feared Zillo Beast, eventually letting the Jedi take it to Coruscant.

KHARRUS

SPECIES: Gran
HEIGHT: 1.78 m (5 ft 10 in)
ALLEGIANCE: Republic
HOMEWORLD: Kinyen

ABILITIES: Diplomacy, politics, legislative knowledge

Senator Kharrus is a veteran diplomat who is familiar with dangerous missions. He is sent to Florrum with a cargo of spice as ransom for Count Dooku, who has been captured by pirates. Unfortunately his transport crashes, and Kharrus dies in the accident.

FINIS VALORUM

SPECIES: Human
HEIGHT: 1.7 m (5 ft 7 in)
ALLEGIANCE: Republic
HOMEWORLD: Coruscant

ABILITIES: Leadership, bureaucracy, legislative strategy, politics, diplomacy

Finis Valorum was the Republic's Chancellor before Palpatine. Now retired, he meets Yoda to solve an old mystery: what became of Jedi Master Sifo-Dyas and Valorum's aide Silman? The answer reveals secrets about the origins of the clones.

MEE DEECHI

SPECIES: Umbaran
HEIGHT: 1.93 m (6 ft 4 in)
ALLEGIANCE: Republic
HOMEWORLD: Umbara

ABILITIES: Politics, legislative strategy, deal-making, ultraviolet vision

Mee Deechi represents Umbara in the Senate and is a strong advocate for military spending. He works with like-minded senators, such as Halle Burtoni, to buy more troops and weapons and give the Republic greater control of the war effort.

SILMAN

SPECIES: Human
HEIGHT: 1.8 m (5 ft 11 in)
ALLEGIANCE: Republic
HOMEWORLD: Coruscant

ABILITIES: Legislative strategy, politics, diplomacy, care of invertebrates

Silman served Chancellor Valorum as an aide and nearly died in the shuttle crash that ended Sifo-Dyas' life. Tossed into prison by the Pykes, a criminal syndicate, Silman goes insane in solitary confinement. Count Dooku kills him to keep the Jedi from learning what he knows.

HALLE BURTONI

SPECIES: Kaminoan
HEIGHT: 2.13 m (7 ft)
ALLEGIANCE: Republic
HOMEWORLD: Kamino

ABILITIES: Political strategy, legislative knowledge, deal-making, diplomacy, leadership

Senator Halle Burtoni represents Kamino, birthplace of the clone army, and does all she can to ensure more clones are produced and credits keep filling Kaminoan coffers. She sees advocates for peace as fools and denounces them in passionate speeches.

KIN ROBB

SPECIES: Human
HEIGHT: 2 m (6 ft 7 in)
ALLEGIANCE: Republic
HOMEWORLD: Taris

ABILITIES: Diplomacy, legislative knowledge, leadership, negotiations

The tall and dignified Senator Kin Robb represents Taris. She is a member of Duchess Satine Kryze's Council of Neutral Systems and allies herself with those seeking a peaceful end to the war, or at least a slowdown in spending on the military and clone production.

SENATE GUARD

SPECIES: Varies
HEIGHT: Varies
ALLEGIANCE: Republic
HOMEWORLD: Varies

ABILITIES: Armed and unarmed combat, security operations

The Senate Guards protect senators and other Republic officials in the galactic capital. Guard membership is considered an honor, and many families have supplied generations of Guards. Service is a proud Coruscanti tradition that dates back centuries.

SENATE COMMANDO

SPECIES: Varies
HEIGHT: Varies
ALLEGIANCE: Republic
HOMEWORLD: Varies

ABILITIES: Armed and unarmed combat, security operations

The bravest members of the Senate Guard are invited to join the group's commando unit, carrying out secret missions on Coruscant and journeying to galactic hot spots to protect key Republic officials.

NIX CARD

SPECIES: Muun
HEIGHT: 2.46 m (8 ft 1 in)
ALLEGIANCE: Banking Clan
HOMEWORLD: Scipio

ABILITIES: Commercial strategy, banking, politics, legislative strategy, dealmaking

The towering Muun Nix Card represents the Banking Clan in the Senate, having stepped in for the disgraced Rush Clovis. Card conspires with Separatist sympathizers in the Senate and Count Dooku to deliver control of the Banking Clan's credits to the shadowy Darth Sidious.

RUSSO-ISC

MODEL: SP-4 ISC crime scene analysis droid
HEIGHT: 1.8 m (5 ft 11 in)
ALLEGIANCE: Jedi Order
MANUFACTURER: Cybot Galactica

ABILITIES: Crime scene analysis, tracking, interrogation, pattern recognition

Russo-ISC is a droid employed by the Jedi Order for specialized work, including analysis of crime scenes. Russo plays a key role in the investigation of the Jedi Temple bombing. He traces the blast to nano-droids and a civilian.

CORUSCANT POLICE DROID

MODEL: GU-series guardian police droid
HEIGHT: 1.8 m (5 ft 11 in)
ALLEGIANCE: Coruscant

MANUFACTURER: SoroSuub Corporation
ABILITIES: Combat, security, interrogation, conflict resolution, speeder piloting

Police droids patrol Coruscant's streets on foot and in speeders, searching for fugitives and keeping the peace. They use batons for most arrests, but have blasters if heavy firepower is needed (as is often the case in the lawless lower levels).

ADMIRAL KILIAN

SPECIES: Human
HEIGHT: 1.72 m (5 ft 8 in)
ALLEGIANCE: Republic

HOMEWORLD: Corellia
ABILITIES: Leadership, diplomacy, military tactics

Admiral Shoan Kilian is commander of the *Endurance* and loyal to his ship, his crew, and the Republic. When young Boba Fett sabotages the *Endurance* over Vanqor, Kilian refuses to abandon his vessel and is taken hostage by Fett and his hunters.

TAN DIVO

SPECIES: Human
HEIGHT: 1.8 m (5 ft 11 in)
ALLEGIANCE: Republic
HOMEWORLD: Coruscant

ABILITIES: Investigations, filling out police reports

Police inspector Tan Divo is called to the Senate Building to solve the death of Senator Onaconda Farr. To his annoyance, he finds plenty of suspects and must deal with interference from nosy Naboo Senator Padmé Amidala.

CORUSCANT UNDERWORLD POLICE

SPECIES: Unknown
HEIGHT: Varies
ALLEGIANCE: Coruscant
HOMEWORLD: Coruscant

ABILITIES: Armed and unarmed combat, tracking, speeder piloting, interrogation, security

The lowest levels of the Coruscant cityscape are extremely dangerous places where arrests are made by the mysterious underworld police. Locals argue about whether these heavily armored figures are droids or living beings. Few have the nerve to get close enough to find out.

AZI-3

MODEL: AZ-series surgical assistant droid
HEIGHT: 0.9 m (2 ft 11 in)
ALLEGIANCE: Kaminoans

MANUFACTURER: Cybot Galactica
ABILITIES: Surgery, biology, medical science, diagnostics, patient care

Nimble fingers useful for data input

AZI-3 is a medical droid who cares for clones in Kamino's Tipoca City production center. He shows great bravery—and a little bit of flexible programming—by helping Fives investigate the inhibitor chips implanted in the clones. This chilling discovery hints at dark secrets about the war. This helpful droid can also transform into a speeder bike.

2-1B-SERIES SURGICAL DROID

MODEL: 2-1B-series surgical droid
HEIGHT: 1.85 m (6 ft 1 in)
ALLEGIANCE: Varies

MANUFACTURER: Industrial Automaton
ABILITIES: Medical science, diagnostics, surgery

2-1B surgical droids serve as doctors throughout the galaxy, and their databases contain information about millions of species. They are designed to interface with shipboard medical scanners, which lets them diagnose injuries remotely, and are programmed to give patients calm reassurance.

R7-A7

MODEL: R-series astromech droid
HEIGHT: 0.96 m (3 ft 2 in)
ALLEGIANCE: Republic
MANUFACTURER: Industrial Automaton

ABILITIES: Starship maintenance, information retrieval, repairs, starfighter piloting

R7-A7 serves as Ahsoka Tano's astromech, flying with her during battles over Ryloth and Umbara. Aboard the *Venator*-class Star Destroyer *Tribunal*, R7-A7 helps her subdue Captain Rex and pushes his programming's limits to remove Rex's inhibitor chip. He soon falls in a firefight with clone troopers.

Onboard logic function displays

RG-G1

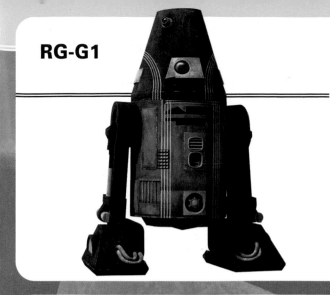

MODEL: R-series astromech droid
HEIGHT: 1.06 m (3 ft 6 in)
ALLEGIANCE: Republic
MANUFACTURER: Industrial Automaton

ABILITIES: Starship maintenance, information retrieval, repairs, starfighter piloting

RG-G1, known as Gee-Gee, serves aboard the *Tribunal*. She joins CH-33P and R7-A7 to help Ahsoka Tano and Captain Rex escape clone troopers obeying Order 66. Gee-Gee keeps the doors to the medical bay sealed while Rex's inhibitor chip is removed.

R6-H5

MODEL: R-series astromech droid
HEIGHT: 0.96 m (3 ft 2 in)
ALLEGIANCE: Republic
MANUFACTURER: Industrial Automaton

ABILITIES: Starship maintenance, information retrieval, repairs, starfighter piloting

R6-H5 serves Kit Fisto and often worries about his master, a habit Fisto finds both endearing and a little annoying. During a mission on Vassek 3, R6 nervously alerts Fisto that General Grievous has arrived in his starfighter and is heading in the Jedi's direction.

CH-33P

Mechanical arm can discharge electricity

MODEL: C1-series astromech droid
HEIGHT: 1.05 m (3 ft 5 in)
ALLEGIANCE: Republic
MANUFACTURER: Industrial Automaton

ABILITIES: Starship maintenance, information retrieval, repairs, starfighter piloting

CH-33P, or Cheep, is an astromech stationed aboard the Star Destroyer *Tribunal* in the final days of the Clone Wars. Cheep and his fellow astromechs help Ahsoka Tano subdue Captain Rex and then join their fight against the clones hunting them throughout the warship.

MEEBUR GASCON

SPECIES: Zilkin
HEIGHT: 0.33 m (1 ft 1 in)
ALLEGIANCE: Republic
HOMEWORLD: Great Zilk

ABILITIES: Military tactics, reconnaissance, infiltration, leadership

Colonel Meebur Gascon is one of the Republic's most determined officers and advises on tactics during the First Battle of Geonosis. He is later tasked with leading D-Squad's droids on a mission to steal a Separatist encryption module. During this dangerous assignment, Gascon rides inside M5-BZ, whose head has been customized to form a command center. Gascon considers himself a brilliant tactician and angrily rejects any suggestion that his record is inflated.

M5-BZ

MODEL: R-series astromech droid
HEIGHT: 1.15 m (3 ft 9 in)
ALLEGIANCE: Jedi Order
MANUFACTURER: Industrial Automaton

ABILITIES: Starship maintenance, information retrieval, repairs, starfighter piloting

M5-BZ serves Jedi Tera Sinube before joining D-Squad for its mission behind enemy lines. His memory banks are removed for the mission to make a space for Meebur Gascon to ride in. M5-BZ later sacrifices himself to save the rest of D-Squad from buzz droids.

QT-KT

MODEL: R-series astromech droid
HEIGHT: 1.09 m (3 ft 7 in)
ALLEGIANCE: Jedi Order
MANUFACTURER: Industrial Automaton

ABILITIES: Starship maintenance, information retrieval, repairs, starfighter piloting, hidden magnetic coil

Magnet can detach and hover independently

QT-KT serves as Jedi Aayla Secura's astromech during the Clone Wars and is loaned out to D-Squad for its infiltration mission. As part of this assignment, QT is upgraded with a powerful magnetic coil built into her dome, which comes in handy on the droids' adventures.

R4-P17

MODEL: R-series astromech droid
HEIGHT: 0.96 m (3 ft 2 in)
ALLEGIANCE: Jedi Order
MANUFACTURER: Industrial Automaton

ABILITIES: Starship maintenance, information retrieval, repairs, starfighter piloting

R4-P17 flies with Obi-Wan Kenobi, sporting a scavenged dome from another unit as a replacement head. R4 is a cautious machine, making her a good companion for Obi-Wan. She survives many missions but is torn apart by buzz droids during the Republic mission to rescue the kidnapped Supreme Chancellor Palpatine.

U9-C4

MODEL: R-series astromech droid
HEIGHT: 1.29 m (4 ft 3 in)
ALLEGIANCE: Jedi Order
MANUFACTURER: Industrial Automaton

ABILITIES: Starship maintenance, information retrieval, repairs, starfighter piloting

Jedi Master Thongla Jur lends his astromech, U9-C4, to D-Squad for its mission. Doctor Gubacher, a research scientist who works for the Jedi Order, adds a powerful laser cutter to C4's set of tools. The attachment can cut through anything, but the downside is it packs a powerful recoil.

> Laser cutter hidden under panel

WAC-47

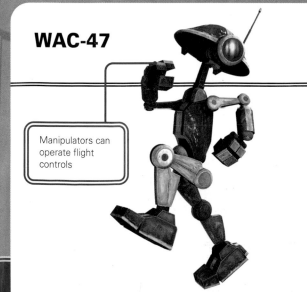

> Manipulators can operate flight controls

MODEL: Modified DUM-series pit droid
HEIGHT: 1.19 m (3 ft 11 in)
ALLEGIANCE: Republic

MANUFACTURER: Serv-O-Droid
ABILITIES: Repairs and maintenance, starship piloting, infiltration

WAC-47 is a modified pit droid who belongs to Commander Neyo and serves as D-Squad's pilot. He is eager to prove his worth and constantly argues with Meebur Gascon about tactics. An apparent glitch prevents him from repeating military titles accurately.

TECKLA MINNAU

SPECIES: Human
HEIGHT: 1.68 m (5 ft 6 in)
ALLEGIANCE: Republic
HOMEWORLD: Naboo

ABILITIES: Armed and unarmed combat, infiltration, security

Teckla Minnau serves Senator Padmé Amidala as a handmaiden and aide. Padmé notes the sacrifices made by Teckla's family in a speech opposing greater military spending. On Scipio, Teckla creates a diversion so Padmé can enter the Banking Clan's vaults. The handmaiden is killed by bounty hunter Embo after completing her mission.

CAPTAIN TYPHO

SPECIES: Human
HEIGHT: 1.85 m (6 ft 1 in)
ALLEGIANCE: Naboo
HOMEWORLD: Naboo

ABILITIES: Armed combat, military tactics, security, starfighter piloting

Gregar Typho is Padmé's head of security, guarding Naboo's senator against her many enemies. His already difficult mission is made harder by Padmé's insistence on putting herself in danger to oppose threats to the Republic and their homeworld. Typho works closely with Padmé's handmaidens to ensure her safety.

HOGAN TINMAR

SPECIES: Human
HEIGHT: 1.83 m (6 ft)
ALLEGIANCE: Naboo

HOMEWORLD: Naboo
ABILITIES: Armed combat, security, airspeeder piloting

Hogan Tinmar is a sergeant in Naboo's Royal Security Forces. He protects Padmé Amidala early in the Clone Wars, often serving as her speeder driver. Tinmar then returns to his homeworld to join Queen Neeyutnee's security detail that protects against the threat of Separatist saboteurs.

SIO BIBBLE

SPECIES: Human
HEIGHT: 1.79 m (5 ft 10 in)
ALLEGIANCE: Naboo
HOMEWORLD: Naboo

ABILITIES: Governance, legislative strategy, diplomacy, leadership, negotiations

Sio Bibble is Naboo's governor and the head of the planet's Royal Advisory Council. He assisted Padmé Amidala when the Trade Federation invaded Naboo and later offers advice to Queens Réillata, Jamillia, and Neeyutnee. Each monarch relies on Bibble to offer plain talk and not useless flattery.

BOSS LYONIE

SPECIES: Gungan
HEIGHT: 2.22 m (7 ft 3 in)
ALLEGIANCE: Gungans
HOMEWORLD: Naboo

ABILITIES: Leadership, diplomacy, negotiations

Boss Lyonie succeeds Boss Nass as head of the Gungan High Council. He maintains the close relationship between the Gungans and the Naboo forged by Nass and Queen Amidala. Lyonie sends Gungan fighters to help the Mon Calamari but is later hypnotized by Rish Loo, a traitorous advisor who is in league with the Separatists.

GENERAL TARPALS

SPECIES: Gungan
HEIGHT: 2.24 m (7 ft 4 in)
ALLEGIANCE: Gungans
HOMEWORLD: Naboo

ABILITIES: Military tactics, armed and unarmed combat, cavalry operations, leadership

Roos Tarpals led Gungan forces in the fight against the Trade Federation and was promoted from captain to general. After Boss Lyonie is tricked into joining the Separatists, Tarpals and Jar Jar Binks pretend to lead an attack on the city of Theed to capture General Grievous. Tarpals sacrifices his life to ensure Grievous' capture.

QUEEN NEEYUTNEE

SPECIES: Human
HEIGHT: 1.69 m (5 ft 7 in)
ALLEGIANCE: Naboo
HOMEWORLD: Naboo

ABILITIES: Leadership, diplomacy, negotiations, legislative knowledge, armed and unarmed combat

Neeyutnee leads Naboo as its queen during much of the Clone Wars. She works closely with Senator Amidala and Representative Jar Jar Binks, as well as Gungan leaders and her Royal Advisory Council. Naboo is a tempting target for Separatist conquest because it's both Padmé and Supreme Chancellor Palpatine's homeworld.

PEPPI BOW

SPECIES: Gungan
HEIGHT: 2.01 m (6 ft 7 in)
ALLEGIANCE: None
HOMEWORLD: Naboo

ABILITIES: Survival, agility, animal care

Gungan Peppi Bow is a herder who watches over her shaaks in the grassy fields of Naboo. When her animals die of a mysterious illness, Peppi sounds the alarm in Theed, with Padmé Amidala and Jar Jar Binks arriving to offer assistance. Peppi helps trace the infection to a Separatist bio-lab hidden in the Eastern Swamps.

ADMIRAL YULAREN

DISCIPLINED LEADER

Rigid stance expected of an officer

Boots kept polished as per regulations

SPECIES: Human
HEIGHT: 1.81 m (5 ft 11 in)
ALLEGIANCE: Republic
HOMEWORLD: Anaxes

ABILITIES: Military tactics, intelligence expert, blaster combat, leadership

A veteran officer, Wullf Yularen is impressed by Anakin Skywalker's Force abilities and skill in battle. However, he is irritated by the Jedi's recklessness and frequent habit of ignoring orders. The efficient Yularen believes a warship's crew should follow its leaders' example and wishes Anakin would set a better one.

"OF ALL THE JEDI, WHY DID I HAVE TO END UP WITH SKYWALKER?"

— Admiral Yularen

AN OLD ENEMY
Yularen discovers that the Separatist blockade of the planet Christophsis is led by Admiral Trench, whom he fought previously at the Battle of Malastare Narrows. Yularen briefs Anakin about Trench's tactics and is impressed when Anakin's unconventional strategy breaks the blockade. Anakin tells Yularen they make a good team.

ADMIRAL TARKIN

A NEW BREED OF OFFICER

SPECIES: Human
HEIGHT: 1.85 m (6 ft 1 in)
ALLEGIANCE: Republic
HOMEWORLD: Eriadu

ABILITIES: Military tactics, leadership, maintaining unwavering dedication to his goals

Ambitious Wilhuff Tarkin serves as captain of Jedi Even Piell's flagship during a mission to secure access to the Nexus Route, a secret hyperspace lane. Tarkin lacks faith in the Jedi, arguing that they should be more ruthless in fighting the war and that the Republic must defeat the Separatists at all costs.

WARTIME PROSECUTOR
Tarkin meets Anakin Skywalker when a Jedi strike team frees him and Even Piell from a Separatist prison on the planet Lola Sayu. After Tarkin's promotion to admiral, he prosecutes Ahsoka Tano for her alleged role in the bombing of the Jedi Temple. Neither Tarkin nor Anakin knows they are fated to meet again.

Republic badge displays military rank

REX

CAPTAIN OF THE 501ST

CC-7567, known as Rex, serves Anakin Skywalker as a captain in the 501st. A gruff, no-nonsense soldier, he values experience over rank and works tirelessly to protect the fellow clones he considers his brothers. As the Clone Wars drag on, Rex comes to see that duty isn't everything and must decide which values are truly worth fighting for.

> ## "IN MY BOOK, EXPERIENCE OUTRANKS EVERYTHING."
>
> – Captain Rex

QUESTIONS OF DESTINY

Rex initially finds Ahsoka Tano brash and immature but comes to respect her determination and appreciate her growth as a leader. His assumptions about duty are shaken by two clones who reject their programming: Slick, who declares that the clones are being used as pawns by the Jedi, and Cut Lawquane, who deserts the army to live as a farmer and father. The clones have been bred to fight, but perhaps there are other options for those brave enough to seize them.

THE CRUCIBLE OF UMBARA

Rex faces a grim test on Umbara, where Jedi General Pong Krell treats his clone troops as disposable, sending them to their deaths. Rex faces a question he's never imagined: is it his duty to obey orders that will only get his brothers killed? The clones outwit Krell and arrest him for treason, but Rex must face a new question: what will happen to the clones when the war ends?

Rangefinder provides tactical analysis

SPECIES: Human (clone)
HEIGHT: 1.83 m (6 ft)
ALLEGIANCE: Republic
HOMEWORLD: Kamino

ABILITIES: Armed and unarmed combat, jetpack expertise, reconnaissance and military tactics, leadership

Rex wields his pistols with style

Phase II clone trooper armor is more adaptable than Phase I armor

TWIN PISTOLS

Rex has a reputation as a solid, dutiful clone commander. In close combat situations he relies on a pair of DC-17 pistols, which he wields with a flair that even Anakin Skywalker has to admire.

TIMELINE

32 BSW4	Born on Kamino
22 BSW4	Fights in the First Battle of Geonosis
22 BSW4	As captain, commands the 501st
22 BSW4	Outwits Slick and arrests him on Christophsis
22 BSW4	Meets Ahsoka Tano during Battle of Christophsis
21 BSW4	Survives snow skirmish with Talz on Orto Plutonia
21 BSW4	Takes part in the Second Battle of Geonosis
21 BSW4	Wounded on Saleucami and meets Cut Lawquane
21 BSW4	Defends clone labs on Kamino
20 BSW4	Arrests Jedi General Pong Krell for treason
19 BSW4	Learns of inhibitor chip conspiracy from Fives
19 BSW4	Fights at Yerbana and is promoted to commander
19 BSW4	Rex's inhibitor chip is removed and he flees the army

FINDING A NEW PATH

When Chancellor Palpatine issues Order 66, Rex's inhibitor chip compels him to obey and target Ahsoka. But Tano saves him, removing the chip and restoring his free will. Rex and Ahsoka survive the horrors of the Jedi Purge and the rise of the Empire, going their separate ways to seek refuge in the Outer Rim. But their friendship endures, and they will meet again.

CODY

LEADER OF THE 212TH ATTACK BATTALION

CC-2224, known as Cody, is a capable clone commander who leads the 212th Attack Battalion and serves as Obi-Wan Kenobi's second-in-command. He forms a close relationship with his Jedi general, who respects Cody for both his tactical abilities and the leadership he shows under fire.

BROTHERS IN ARMS
Cody is a friend of Captain Rex, who serves Obi-Wan's former Padawan, Anakin Skywalker. The two work together to outthink the traitorous clone Sergeant Slick, lead a unit of rookies against a Separatist attack on the Rishi Moon, and team up to defend their homeworld, Kamino, when it's invaded. Both continue to do their duty even as too many of their clone brothers fall in battle and become casualties of war.

SPECIALIZED EQUIPMENT
Cody's armor displays the orange flares of the 212th. His helmet is enhanced with a visor to reduce glare, and his equipment includes backup communications antennae. Cody also wears a jetpack for aerial maneuvers.

SPECIES: Human (clone)	ABILITIES: Armed and unarmed
HEIGHT: 1.83 m (6 ft)	combat, jetpack expertise,
ALLEGIANCE: Republic	reconnaissance, leadership,
HOMEWORLD: Kamino	military tactics

Secondary antenna for communications during operations

A BY-THE-BOOK SOLDIER

Cody is bold on the battlefield but dutiful away from it, often quoting regulations to troopers who fail to follow procedure. He sometimes wonders how Rex can stand serving a Jedi as reckless as Anakin and is grateful that Obi-Wan is more cautious in battle than his old Padawan.

Few Jedi commanders and clone officers develop a bond as close as the one that forms between Cody and Obi-Wan over many battles during the Clone Wars. Obi-Wan comes to trust that Cody will never let him down, while Cody and the troops under his command respect their Jedi general's skill as both a negotiator and a warrior.

TIMELINE

32 BSW4	Born on Kamino
22 BSW4	Apprehends clone traitor Slick on Christophsis
21 BSW4	Takes part in the Second Battle of Geonosis
21 BSW4	Plays key role in clone defense of Kamino
20 BSW4	Fights with ground forces during the Battle of Umbara
19 BSW4	Joins hunt for Maul after the Battle of Ord Mantell
19 BSW4	Injured in Quinlan Vos' escape from custody
19 BSW4	Assists Rex during the Battle of Anaxes
19 BSW4	Leads ground units at the Battle of Yerbana
19 BSW4	Accompanies Obi-Wan Kenobi to Utapau to confront General Grievous
19 BSW4	Obeys Order 66 and orders strike on Obi-Wan

DC-15 rifle fires charged plasma bolts

"SOMETIMES IN WAR IT'S HARD TO BE THE ONE WHO SURVIVES."

– Commander Cody

WOLFFE

ALPHA OF THE WOLFPACK

Cybernetic eye replaces one lost fighting Asajj Ventress

Helmet and armor display wolf markings

SPECIES: Human (clone)
HEIGHT: 1.83 m (6 ft)
ALLEGIANCE: Republic
HOMEWORLD: Kamino

ABILITIES: Combat, military tactics, leadership

CC-3636, also known as Wolffe, serves Jedi Master Plo Koon as commander of the Wolfpack, a close-knit squad of highly effective troopers known for their ferocity in battle. Wolffe and his squad mates are devoted to their Jedi general, knowing he would do anything to preserve their lives on the battlefield.

"COMMANDER, WE ARE TAKING YOU IN."

– Commander Wolffe

HUNTING A FUGITIVE

After the bombing of Coruscant's Jedi Temple, Wolffe leads a shock trooper squad in search of Ahsoka Tano, who is considered a fugitive from justice. Ahsoka once saved the lives of Wolffe and his squad at Abregado, but orders are orders, and the veteran clone trooper is determined to obey them.

GREGOR

MYSTERIOUS EXILE

SPECIES: Human (clone)
HEIGHT: 1.83 m (6 ft)
ALLEGIANCE: Republic
HOMEWORLD: Kamino

ABILITIES: Armed and unarmed combat, military tactics, restaurant sanitation

Clone commando CC-5576-39 disappears during the Battle of Sarrish and is considered dead. But the former officer survives, winding up on the Outer Rim planet Abafar with no memory of his past. Using the name Gregor, he works as a dishwasher in a diner—at least until a Republic squad discovers him.

REJOINING THE FIGHT
Republic Colonel Meebur Gascon helps Gregor recover his true identity. After reclaiming his armor and weapons from the diner owner who stole them, Gregor helps Gascon and D-Squad leave Abafar. Covering their escape, Gregor dispatches many battle droids and is assumed to die in an explosion. But clone commandos are hard to kill, and Gregor's story isn't over.

Tally of defeated droids

Camo printing on *Katarn*-class armor

ECHO

SEPARATIST PRISONER

SPECIES: Human (clone)
HEIGHT: 1.85 m (6 ft 1 in)
ALLEGIANCE: Republic
HOMEWORLD: Kamino

ABILITIES: Combat training, military tactics, cybernetic implants

CT-1409, or Echo, proves himself fighting off a Separatist raid on the Rishi Moon and defending Kamino. Echo is promoted to ARC trooper, but he is believed to have been killed during a mission to Lola Sayu. However, he is still alive and is a Separatist prisoner, turned into a cyborg so his knowledge can be used against the Republic.

A CRUEL EXPERIMENT

During a mission on Anaxes, Rex learns that Echo is alive and is being held prisoner on Skako Minor. He has been cybernetically rebuilt and trapped in a stasis tank. Once freed, Echo helps the Republic win a key victory at Anaxes and decides to join the band of aberrant clone commandos known as the Bad Batch.

"ECHO'S FINGERPRINTS ARE ALL OVER THESE SEPARATIST STRATEGIES."

– Captain Rex

FIVES

SEEKER OF SECRETS

Double pauldron indicates rank and specialist status

Blast-resistant kama prevents combat injuries

SPECIES: Human (clone)
HEIGHT: 1.83 m (6 ft)
ALLEGIANCE: Republic
HOMEWORLD: Kamino

ABILITIES: Combat training, military tactics, reconnaissance

After completing cadet training, CT-5555 is sent to the Rishi Moon and immediately tested when Separatists raid the outpost. Fives fights well and is promoted to ARC trooper after defending Kamino. He serves with distinction at Lola Sayu and Umbara, but a strange incident at Ringo Vinda changes his life, leaving him struggling with questions about the war and his duty.

> "THE MISSION ... THE NIGHTMARES ... THEY'RE FINALLY OVER."
>
> – Fives

DREADFUL DISCOVERY

After clone trooper Tup shoots his Jedi general at the Battle of Ringo Vinda, Fives learns that every clone has an inhibitor chip implanted in his brain. He tells the Jedi and the Republic what he's found, but few believe his story, and his attempt to unravel the conspiracy ends tragically.

HUNTER

BAD BATCH'S SERGEANT

Backpack contains mission-critical equipment

Ideal weapon for stealth missions

SPECIES: Human (clone)
HEIGHT: 1.8 m (5 ft 11 in)
ALLEGIANCE: Republic
HOMEWORLD: Kamino

ABILITIES: Enhanced senses, specialist training, superior hand-to-hand combatant, leadership

A mutated clone, Hunter is in charge of the infamous commando unit known officially as Clone Force 99 and unofficially as the Bad Batch. Besides possessing a talent for leadership, Hunter can sense droids' electromagnetic fields—an invaluable ability given that his unit is often sent on dangerous, top-secret missions.

"WHAT KIND OF SUICIDE MISSION DO YOU HAVE FOR US THIS TIME?"

– Hunter

HUNT FOR THE ALGORITHM
Hunter is reluctant to work with Rex's regular clones on a mission to infiltrate a Separatist outpost on Anaxes. The "regs," he fears, will just get in the way of the Bad Batch and its unusual—and effective—combat tactics. But the mission teaches Hunter to respect Rex as a leader and a surprisingly creative thinker.

CROSSHAIR

ELITE MARKSMAN

SPECIES: Human (clone)
HEIGHT: 1.93 m (6 ft 4 in)
ALLEGIANCE: Republic
HOMEWORLD: Kamino
ABILITIES: Combat abilities, sharpshooting, superior vision

Crosshair is another mutated clone member of the Bad Batch. He has vision far superior to a regular clone's, allowing him to hit targets at almost unbelievable distances with his sniper rifle. Crosshair is utterly devoted to marksmanship: his helmet is modified so he can fit his 773 Firepuncher rifle's scope against his eyepiece, and he has crosshairs tattooed across his right eye.

COLD-HEARTED MAN

Crosshair has an icy personality and can be cynical and bitter about the war. While dedicated to his colleagues in the Bad Batch, he has little regard for regular clones, whom he views as expendable. On Skako Minor, Crosshair's attitude sparks an angry confrontation with Captain Rex.

"WHEN YOU HAVE TO HIT A PRECISE TARGET FROM 10 KLICKS, CROSSHAIR'S YOUR MAN."

– Hunter

773 Firepuncher rifle is a favorite of Republic snipers

DC-17 blaster pistol used as secondary weapon

WRECKER

CLONE BERSERKER

Ominous helmet strikes fear in enemies

Excellent tool for cutting off stingers

SPECIES: Human (clone)
HEIGHT: 1.98 m (6 ft 6 in)
ALLEGIANCE: Republic
HOMEWORLD: Kamino

ABILITIES: Enormous strength, armed and unarmed combat

Wrecker is a mutated clone whose immense strength makes him the muscle of the Bad Batch squad. He loves combat, takes delight in reducing droids to scrap, and blowing things up—the bigger the bang, the happier he is. Wrecker has a dark, twisted sense of humor, but he's fiercely loyal to his fellow Clone Force 99 clones and anyone else whose ability to fight proves worthy of his respect.

"THE CAVALRY HAS ARRIVED!"

— Wrecker

MAYHEM ON ANAXES

The Anaxes campaign is great fun for Wrecker, who gets to lift gunship wreckage, destroy lots of droids, damage Separatist equipment, and cause the kind of mayhem he likes best. At the battle's climax, Anakin Skywalker lets Wrecker blow up an entire Separatist battleship. The massive commando has rarely been so happy.

TECH

GENIUS SOLDIER

SPECIES: Human (clone)
HEIGHT: 1.93 m (6 ft 4 in)
ALLEGIANCE: Republic
HOMEWORLD: Kamino

ABILITIES: Technical abilities, slicing, decryption, language skill, armed and unarmed combat, military tactics, gift for improvisation

The lanky, brainy clone named Tech is the Bad Batch's resident genius. He is an expert slicer and problem solver who prefers clever planning to brute force in defeating the Republic's enemies. He has computer terminals built into his armor and his helmet's visor, allowing him instant access to information that he uses to give his fellow clones the edge in battle.

HEARING AN ECHO
Tech plays a critical role in tracing the origins of a mysterious Separatist algorithm to Skako Minor and in rescuing the ARC trooper Echo from his captors. He then helps the Bad Batch escape a Separatist facility by using a recording of keeradaks to summon the flying creatures. The clones then use the winged beasts to ride off into the skies.

"I DO HAVE A BRILLIANT IDEA."

— Tech

Visor displays computer readout

FOX

SPECIES: Human (clone)
HEIGHT: 1.83 m (6 ft)
ALLEGIANCE: Republic
HOMEWORLD: Kamino

ABILITIES: Combat abilities, military tactics, leadership, reconnaissance, riot control

"STAND DOWN! STAND DOWN! GET ON YOUR KNEES!"

– Commander Fox

CC-1010, called Fox, leads the elite unit known as the Coruscant Guard. The group protects members of the Senate and the Supreme Chancellor, helps keep the peace in the Republic capital, and tracks down dangerous fugitives. Fox's quarries include Ziro the Hutt, Ahsoka Tano, and the renegade clone trooper Fives, who flees from the Grand Republic Medical Facility after apparently trying to kill Palpatine. Obeying orders, Fox fires the shot that ends Fives' life.

BLY

SPECIES: Human (clone)
HEIGHT: 1.83 m (6 ft)
ALLEGIANCE: Republic
HOMEWORLD: Kamino

ABILITIES: Combat abilities, military tactics, leadership, aerial maneuvers, reconnaissance

CC-5052, or Bly, is a veteran commander of many battles with the 327th Star Corps. He serves under Aayla Secura and has formed a close bond with his Jedi general. Bly fights alongside Aayla, Anakin Skywalker, Ahsoka Tano, and Captain Rex at the Battle of Quell and after a party of Jedi and clones are marooned on Maridun. Bly respects Aayla for her grit in battle and for her sense of duty: she doesn't let personal feelings get in the way of a mission. He must do the same on Felucia when Aayla becomes a target of Order 66.

"GENERAL SECURA, WE HAVE A PROBLEM."

– Commander Bly

Macrobinocs used for reconnaissance

GREE

SPECIES: Human (clone)
HEIGHT: 1.83 m (6 ft)
ALLEGIANCE: Republic
HOMEWORLD: Kamino

ABILITIES: Combat abilities, military tactics, leadership, aerial maneuvers, data-slicing, reconnaissance, infiltration

> **"YOU AND I DISAGREE ON WHAT MAKES A GOOD SOLDIER."**
>
> – Commander Gree

CC-1004, called Gree, commands the 41st Elite Corps, led by Luminara Unduli. Like his Jedi general, Gree is a careful, by-the-book soldier who doesn't believe in cutting corners. Gree is assigned to guard Separatist leader Nute Gunray for transport back to Coruscant after his capture on Rodia. The clone brawls with Senate Commando Captain Argyus when he betrays the Republic and frees Gunray. Gree later fights at the Second Battle of Geonosis and on Kashyyyk, where he confronts Yoda during Order 66. The Jedi Grandmaster ends Gree's life with a swipe of his lightsaber's green blade.

Bandolier holds extra ammunition

PONDS

SPECIES: Human (clone)
HEIGHT: 1.83 m (6 ft)
ALLEGIANCE: Republic
HOMEWORLD: Kamino

ABILITIES: Combat abilities, leadership, military tactics, reconnaissance

> **"I HAVE FIVE SPECIAL COMMANDO UNITS AWAITING YOUR ORDERS, SIR."**
>
> – Commander Ponds

DCA-15 rifle is effective at long range

CT-411, known as Ponds, serves under the Jedi General Mace Windu. He is a veteran commander of many battles, including Geonosis, Ryloth, and Malastare. Ponds is an expert at reconnaissance, leading Lightning Squadron's ARF troopers on Ryloth. The back of his helmet bears a cheerful stenciled message to anyone following him into battle: some guys have all the luck. Ponds is taken hostage in bounty hunter Boba Fett's raid on the Star Destroyer *Endurance* and killed by Fett's ruthless mentor Aurra Sing to show Windu that Fett means business. Windu witnesses the loyal soldier's tragic fate with quiet anger.

NEYO

SPECIES: Human (clone)
HEIGHT: 1.83 m (6 ft)
ALLEGIANCE: Republic
HOMEWORLD: Kamino

ABILITIES: Armed and unarmed combat, military tactics, reconnaissance, speeder piloting

Symbol of the 91st Reconnaissance Force

CC-8826, known as Neyo, is a clone commander who lends his pit droid, WAC-47, to D-Squad. His generosity is rewarded, as the droid foils a Separatist attack on the Valor, a Republic space station, while Neyo is aboard. He later fights on Saleucami during the Outer Rim Sieges with Jedi Master Stass Allie.

JET

SPECIES: Human (clone)
HEIGHT: 1.83 m (6 ft)
ALLEGIANCE: Republic
HOMEWORLD: Kamino

ABILITIES: Starfighter and starship piloting, military tactics

CC-1993, nicknamed Jet, serves under Jedi General Ki-Adi-Mundi. During the Second Battle of Geonosis, Jet leads squads of flametroopers through hives crowded with Geonosian drones. The clone commander and his troops must fight for every meter of ground but manage to complete their mission.

ODD BALL

SPECIES: Human (clone)
HEIGHT: 1.83 m (6 ft)
ALLEGIANCE: Republic
HOMEWORLD: Kamino

ABILITIES: Starfighter and starship piloting, military tactics

The veteran clone pilot CC-2237, known as Odd Ball, often flies with Obi-Wan Kenobi. The clone's long record of missions includes Teth, Umbara, and Cato Neimoidia. Odd Ball nearly dies at Teth, but Obi-Wan saves his V-19 Torrent fighter from vulture droid attackers.

HAVOC

SPECIES: Human (clone)
HEIGHT: 1.83 m (6 ft)
ALLEGIANCE: Republic
HOMEWORLD: Kamino

ABILITIES: Armed and unarmed combat, military tactics

Clone trooper Havoc proves himself as a soldier and is rewarded with a promotion to ARC trooper. He serves in Rancor Battalion with Commander Colt and checks in on clone cadets' training on the world Kamino. Havoc dies defending Tipoca City against Separatist invaders.

Ammo cartridges

APPO

SPECIES: Human (clone)
HEIGHT: 1.83 m (6 ft)
ALLEGIANCE: Republic
HOMEWORLD: Kamino

ABILITIES: Armed and unarmed combat, military tactics, reconnaissance, peacekeeping

Appo's armor markings are common across Anakin's unit

CC-1119, or Appo, is a sergeant in Anakin Skywalker's 501st during the campaign on Umbara and is promoted to commander afterward. When Anakin splits up his troops so half of them can join the Siege of Mandalore, Appo is placed in command of the other group heading to Coruscant. During Order 66, Appo and fallen Jedi Anakin attack the Jedi Temple.

MONNK

SPECIES: Human (clone)
HEIGHT: 1.83 m (6 ft)
ALLEGIANCE: Republic
HOMEWORLD: Kamino

ABILITIES: Armed and unarmed combat, military tactics, aquatic maneuvers

Monnk commands clone SCUBA troops on the watery world Mon Cala and reports to Jedi Master Kit Fisto. Monnk, Fisto, and their troops arrive just in time to save Mon Cala's Prince Lee-Char from being wiped out by Separatist and Quarren forces, then wage a guerrilla war against the attackers.

TUP

SPECIES: Human (clone)
HEIGHT: 1.83 m (6 ft)
ALLEGIANCE: Republic
HOMEWORLD: Kamino

ABILITIES: Armed and unarmed combat, reconnaissance, military tactics

CT-5385, known as Tup, is a young clone assigned to the 501st. On Umbara, he quickly proves cool under fire, earning the respect of Captain Rex, Fives, and other veteran soldiers. He helps devise the clones' plan to capture Jedi General Pong Krell, preventing Krell from killing more troopers. During the Battle of Ringo Vinda, Tup suddenly shoots Tiplar, his Jedi General, while mumbling that "good soldiers follow orders." This shocking act is traced to a malfunctioning inhibitor chip in Tup's brain. Tup dies shortly after the chip is removed.

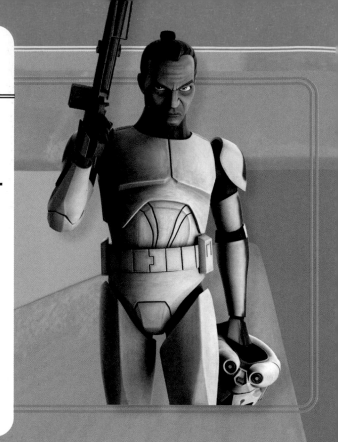

Symbol of Republic Medic Corps

KIX

SPECIES: Human (clone)
HEIGHT: 1.83 m (6 ft)
ALLEGIANCE: Republic
HOMEWORLD: Kamino

ABILITIES: Medical training, armed and unarmed combat, reconnaissance, military tactics

CT-6116, or Kix, is a clone medic who serves with the 501st. He has been trained to handle everything from minor injuries to life-threatening wounds. Kix races fearlessly around the battlefield with medpacs, pain stims, and anything else that might save the lives of his clone brothers.

Kix fights in multiple battles including Saleucami, Kiros, Umbara, and Ringo Vinda. While hunting General Grievous on Saleucami, he saves Captain Rex's life and reminds his reluctant superior officer that a medic outranks everyone when it comes to health.

HEVY

SPECIES: Human (clone)	**ABILITIES:** Armed and
HEIGHT: 1.83 m (6 ft)	unarmed combat, heavy
ALLEGIANCE: Republic	weapons expert, military
HOMEWORLD: Kamino	tactics, reconnaissance

CT-782 is a member of Domino Squad and is given his nickname Hevy by Clone 99 because of his training in heavy weapons, such as the Z-6 rotary blaster cannon. Clone 99 plays a key role in persuading the Dominos to work as a team and complete their cadet training on Kamino.

Hevy's life proves tragically short: he is assigned to the Rishi Station listening post as a "shiny," or new clone trooper. When Separatist commando droids attack the station, Hevy sacrifices his life to destroy the listening post and its invaders.

JESSE

SPECIES: Human (clone)	**ABILITIES:** Armed and
HEIGHT: 1.83 m (6 ft)	unarmed combat, military
ALLEGIANCE: Republic	tactics
HOMEWORLD: Kamino	

CT-5597, known as Jesse, fights with the 501st, seeing action at Saleucami, Umbara, Ringo Vinda, Anaxes, and during the Siege of Mandalore. He proves himself highly capable in combat and is promoted to ARC trooper before the end of the war. The Republic sigil adorns his face and helmet.

When the clones receive Order 66, Jesse is unable to resist his conditioning and apprehends Captain Rex and Ahsoka Tano in the *Tribunal*'s hangar bay, seeking to bring them to justice as traitors against the Republic. Jesse dies during the attempt.

BOIL

SPECIES: Human (clone)
HEIGHT: 1.83 m (6 ft)
ALLEGIANCE: Republic
HOMEWORLD: Kamino

ABILITIES: Armed and unarmed combat, reconnaissance, infiltration, military tactics

Helmet hides well-groomed mustache

Boil is a member of Ghost Company who sees combat on Ryloth, Geonosis, Kiros, and Christophsis. He is skilled at reconnaissance and infiltration, and these abilities prove vital in freeing Ryloth from Separatist leader Wat Tambor. He and fellow clone Waxer become close friends during the conflict.

On Ryloth, Boil at first calls the planet's Twi'leks "tail-heads." But he comes to care for an orphaned girl, named Numa, and to understand what the Republic fights for. Boil's helmet bears a cartoon of Numa as a reminder for the rest of the war.

WAXER

SPECIES: Human (clone)
HEIGHT: 1.83 m (6 ft)
ALLEGIANCE: Republic
HOMEWORLD: Kamino

ABILITIES: Armed and unarmed combat, reconnaissance, infiltration, military tactics

Clone trooper Waxer serves with Boil in Ghost Company, helping save Numa on Ryloth and liberate the planet's Twi'leks. He is promoted to lieutenant later in the war and leads troops in the difficult campaign to free the planet Umbara from the Separatists. During the fight, General Pong Krell sends Waxer's platoon into combat against other clone units. He is mortally wounded but is able to tell Rex of Krell's treacherous act.

DOGMA

SPECIES: Human (clone)
HEIGHT: 1.83 m (6 ft)
ALLEGIANCE: Republic
HOMEWORLD: Kamino

ABILITIES: Armed and unarmed combat, military tactics

Dogma is a stern young clone trooper assigned to the 501st under Captain Rex. Many of Rex's veterans have learned that war calls for a certain flexibility, but Dogma rejects this, arguing that orders must be followed instantly and without question.

When Pong Krell begins sending the 501st into harm's way, Dogma at first defends the Jedi general. But when Krell causes clones to fire on each other, something in Dogma snaps. He shoots Krell dead, unwilling to wait for a military trial.

Cadet helmet needs a good polishing

CLONE 99

SPECIES: Human (clone)
HEIGHT: 1.68 m (5 ft 6 in)
ALLEGIANCE: Republic
HOMEWORLD: Kamino

ABILITIES: Sanitation, military tactics, leadership

Accidents in clone production can lead to mutations, such as the ones that leave Clone 99 unable to fight, and he instead works as a janitor on Kamino. Clone 99 takes pride in his clone heritage and supports clone cadets as they struggle with the demands of army training.

Clone 99 inspires Domino Squad to work as a team, then assists the clone army when Separatist droids invade Kamino. He dies fetching ammunition during this battle but is not forgotten: Clone Force 99, a unit of mutated clones, is named in his memory.

HAWK

SPECIES: Human (clone)
HEIGHT: 1.83 m (6 ft)
ALLEGIANCE: Republic
HOMEWORLD: Kamino

ABILITIES: Gunship piloting, starfighter piloting, military tactics

Hawk flies a gunship in many battles, from Christophsis to Scipio. Gunship pilots need steely nerves, as they must fly their transports in and out of heavy fire zones and remain on the ground while troops load and unload.

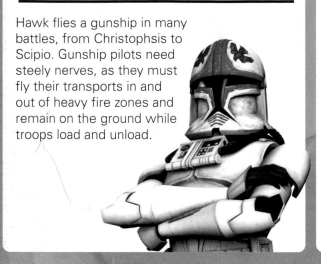

CHOPPER

SPECIES: Human (clone)
HEIGHT: 1.83 m (6 ft)
ALLEGIANCE: Republic
HOMEWORLD: Kamino

ABILITIES: Armed and unarmed combat, repairs

Squad mates of Chopper admit he's a little weird: he collects fingers of battle droids as trophies. When the Republic learns there's a traitor in Sergeant Slick's squad, suspicion falls on Chopper. But he's proven innocent.

HARDCASE

SPECIES: Human (clone)
HEIGHT: 1.83 m (6 ft)
ALLEGIANCE: Republic
HOMEWORLD: Kamino

ABILITIES: Armed and unarmed combat, heavy weaponry, military tactics

Hardcase fights in battles including Mimban, Saleucami, and Umbara. He's an expert with a Z-6 rotary cannon. It's the perfect weapon for Hardcase, who's always eager for battle and claims he's hyperactive due to a leak in his growth acceleration chamber.

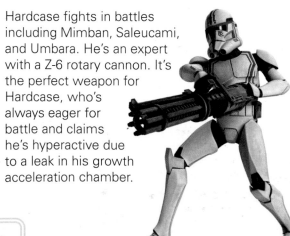

DROIDBAIT

SPECIES: Human (clone)
HEIGHT: 1.83 m (6 ft)
ALLEGIANCE: Republic
HOMEWORLD: Kamino

ABILITIES: Armed and unarmed combat, military tactics

CT-00-2010 earns the nickname Droidbait as a cadet after grumbling that Domino Squad uses him to draw out mechanical foes. His nickname turns out to be grimly prophetic, as he is killed by commando droids that infiltrate the Republic's outpost on the Rishi Moon.

SINKER

SPECIES: Human (clone)
HEIGHT: 1.83 m (6 ft)
ALLEGIANCE: Republic
HOMEWORLD: Kamino

ABILITIES: Armed and unarmed combat, military tactics

Sinker is a veteran sergeant in Plo Koon's famed Wolfpack battalion. He survives being hunted by the Separatist cruiser *Malevolence* to fight on worlds such as Felucia and Aleen. Sinker later joins Plo Koon to investigate a mysterious distress call originating on Oba Diah's moon.

O'NINER

SPECIES: Human (clone)
HEIGHT: 1.83 m (6 ft)
ALLEGIANCE: Republic
HOMEWORLD: Kamino

ABILITIES: Armed and unarmed combat, military tactics, leadership

O'Niner is a clone sergeant in charge of the Republic listening post on the Rishi Moon. His squad is made up of "shinies," rookie troopers fresh from training on Kamino. O'Niner dies when Separatist commando droids overrun the outpost.

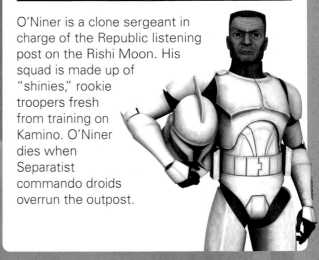

BRIC

SPECIES: Siniteen
HEIGHT: 1.91 m (6 ft 3 in)
ALLEGIANCE: Republic
HOMEWORLD: Mileva

ABILITIES: Military tactics, leadership, infiltration, tracking, reconnaissance

The hard-nosed bounty hunter named Bric helps the Republic train clone cadets on Kamino. He is a tough taskmaster with little patience for trainees who don't meet his high standards. His bullying is in contrast with the kindness shown by El-Les.

EL-LES

SPECIES: Arcona
HEIGHT: 1.83 m (6 ft)
ALLEGIANCE: Republic
HOMEWORLD: Cona

ABILITIES: Military tactics, leadership, tracking, reconnaissance

El-Les is an Arcona mercenary who teams up with Bric to train clone cadets for the Republic, taking a gentler approach to teaching than his partner. El-Les tries to help the cadets of Domino Squad when they struggle to master their military training on Kamino.

BOSS

SPECIES: Human (clone)
HEIGHT: 1.83 m (6 ft)
ALLEGIANCE: Republic
HOMEWORLD: Kamino

ABILITIES: Leadership, armed and unarmed combat, military tactics, infiltration, reconnaissance, sniper skills, jetpack training

RC-1138, known as Boss, is a sergeant who leads the elite commando unit known as Delta Squad for some of the war's most dangerous missions. Boss leads Delta Squad's search for survivors after Savage Opress' raid on Devaron's ancient Temple of Eedit.

FIXER

SPECIES: Human (clone)
HEIGHT: 1.83 m (6 ft)
ALLEGIANCE: Republic
HOMEWORLD: Kamino

ABILITIES: Slicer skills, armed and unarmed combat, military tactics, infiltration, reconnaissance, mechanical repairs, jetpack training

RC-1140 is Boss' second-in-command in Delta Squad. He is known as Fixer because of his skills as a slicer and tinkerer. Fixer is quiet, grim, and so focused on following regulations that he uses his comrades' operating numbers during missions.

SCORCH

SPECIES: Human (clone)
HEIGHT: 1.83 m (6 ft)
ALLEGIANCE: Republic
HOMEWORLD: Kamino

ABILITIES: Armed and unarmed combat, military tactics, infiltration, reconnaissance, demolition, jetpack training

RC-1262, nicknamed Scorch, is an elite commando who acts as Delta Squad's explosives expert. Scorch is quick with a joke even when combat is at its hottest. He is frustrated to find nothing to blow up when the Deltas survey the aftermath of Savage Opress' attack on a Jedi temple.

SEV

SPECIES: Human (clone)
HEIGHT: 1.83 m (6 ft)
ALLEGIANCE: Republic
HOMEWORLD: Kamino

ABILITIES: Armed and unarmed combat, military tactics, infiltration, reconnaissance, tracking, jetpack training, sniper skills

RC-1207, nicknamed Sev, is a commando in Delta Squad. Sev is the unit's sniper, and his many skills include tracking and survival. Sev seems to love combat, and his enthusiasm for battle can strike his fellow Deltas as a bit disturbing.

THIRE

SPECIES: Human (clone)
HEIGHT: 1.83 m (6 ft)
ALLEGIANCE: Republic
HOMEWORLD: Kamino

ABILITIES: Armed and unarmed combat, military tactics

CC-4477, known as Thire, is a lieutenant in the Coruscant Guard. On Rugosa, Yoda urges Thire to stay positive even when facing terrible odds and advises him not to rush into fights. After Order 66, Thire helps Darth Sidious hunt for Yoda following the Jedi and Sith duel in the grand Senate Chamber on Coruscant.

JEK

SPECIES: Human (clone)
HEIGHT: 1.83 m (6 ft)
ALLEGIANCE: Republic
HOMEWORLD: Kamino

ABILITIES: Armed and unarmed combat, military tactics, heavy weaponry, reconnaissance, tracking

Jek is part of the Coruscant Guard. He relies on his Z-6 rotary cannon in battle, but Yoda encourages him to think of his mind as a tool more powerful than any weapon. Jek follows the Jedi Master's advice and retrains as a scout. He later serves in the Battle of Kashyyyk under Commander Gree.

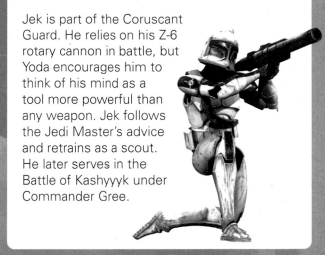

RYS

SPECIES: Human (clone)
HEIGHT: 1.83 m (6 ft)
ALLEGIANCE: Republic
HOMEWORLD: Kamino

ABILITIES: Armed and unarmed combat, military tactics, security

Rys is a member of the Coruscant Guard. He travels with Yoda to Rugosa and learns a valuable lesson from the Jedi: to draw inspiration from his fellow clones. Rys survives Rugosa, but Yoda has a vision of the clone's death later in the war.

JAX

SPECIES: Human (clone)
HEIGHT: 1.44 m (4 ft 9 in)
ALLEGIANCE: Republic
HOMEWORLD: Kamino

ABILITIES: Military tactics, developing leadership skills

Jax is a clone cadet and a leader in the Clone Youth Brigade. While on a training mission onboard the *Endurance*, Jax befriends a cadet known as Lucky. Jax is unaware that his friend is really Boba Fett, who plans to destroy the warship as part of his plan to kill Mace Windu.

CLONE TROOPER

SPECIES: Human (clone)
HEIGHT: 1.83 m (6 ft)
ALLEGIANCE: Republic
HOMEWORLD: Kamino

ABILITIES: Armed and unarmed combat, military tactics

The clone troopers of the Grand Army of the Republic are genetically identical soldiers designed and grown by Kaminoan cloners. These troops are critical in defending Republic worlds from Separatist droid armies. Each clone has an inhibitor chip in his brain to ensure obedience.

ARC TROOPER

SPECIES: Human (clone)
HEIGHT: 1.83 m (6 ft)
ALLEGIANCE: Republic
HOMEWORLD: Kamino

ABILITIES: Armed and unarmed combat, military tactics, leadership, survival, infiltration, reconnaissance

Advanced Recon Commandos are elite clone troops who often lead soldiers into battle as officers. Some are trained for ARC responsibilities as cadets on Kamino. Others are chosen from the ranks of regular clone units after proving their bravery and ingenuity on the battlefield.

ARF TROOPER

SPECIES: Human (clone)
HEIGHT: 1.83 m (6 ft)
ALLEGIANCE: Republic
HOMEWORLD: Kamino

ABILITIES Armed and unarmed combat, military tactics, cavalry operations, reconnaissance

Advanced Recon Force troopers are the cavalry of the Republic army, riding AT-RTs on scouting missions and in battle. Clones with exceptional agility are given ARF training, and such troopers regard themselves as a breed apart. They see piloting an AT-RT as more like riding a living mount than driving a vehicle.

CLONE PILOT

SPECIES: Human (clone)
HEIGHT: 1.83 m (6 ft)
ALLEGIANCE: Republic
HOMEWORLD: Kamino

ABILITIES: Armed and unarmed combat, military tactics, survival, starfighter/ starship piloting

Clone pilots can fly anything, from transports to starfighters. Any clone cadets with exceptional reflexes and vision are identified early on Kamino and given specialized training, with those who make the grade "earning their wings" as pilo.

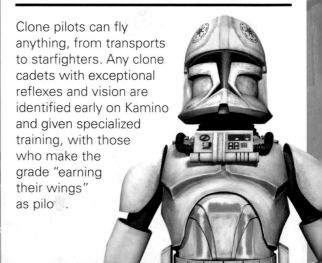

BARC TROOPER

SPECIES: Human (clone)
HEIGHT: 1.83 m (6 ft)
ALLEGIANCE: Republic
HOMEWORLD: Kamino

ABILITIES: Armed and unarmed combat, military tactics, reconnaissance, speeder piloting

BARC troopers are specialized ARC units trained to pilot speeder bikes. They are often assigned reconnaissance missions but can also act as cavalry for their allies or as a vanguard for ARF troopers on AT-RTs. BARC troopers excel at high-speed combat and boast that they have the speediest reaction times in the clone army.

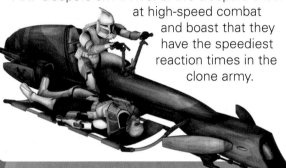

SHOCK TROOPER

SPECIES: Human (clone)
HEIGHT: 1.83 m (6 ft)
ALLEGIANCE: Republic
HOMEWORLD: Kamino

ABILITIES: Armed and unarmed combat, military tactics, security, riot control

The clone troopers of the Coruscant Guard are also known as shock troopers. They can be recognized by their armor's red markings: in the Republic, red has been a sign of diplomatic status for millennia. Shock troopers protect the Chancellor, senators, and other vital personnel.

ORDNANCE TROOPER

SPECIES: Human (clone)
HEIGHT: 1.83 m (6 ft)
ALLEGIANCE: Republic
HOMEWORLD: Kamino

ABILITIES: Armed and unarmed combat, military tactics, explosives handling, infiltration, security

Ordnance specialists have one of the most dangerous jobs in the Republic military: defusing bombs. Clones chosen for this perilous work must have steady nerves, a gentle touch, and be able to focus amid the chaos of war. They play a key role in disarming bombs on Naboo.

CLONE SCUBA TROOPER

SPECIES: Human (clone)
HEIGHT: 1.83 m (6 ft)
ALLEGIANCE: Republic
HOMEWORLD: Kamino

ABILITIES: Armed and unarmed combat, underwater maneuvers, survival, infiltration, sub piloting

Clone SCUBA troopers are soldiers trained for underwater combat. They use specialized gear including fins, breathing tubes, and blasters equipped with lights. Many of these soldiers are taught to pilot speedy Devilfish subs. Clone SCUBA troopers play a vital part in the Republic's defense of Mon Cala.

COLD ASSAULT TROOPER

SPECIES: Human (clone)
HEIGHT: 1.83 m (6 ft)
ALLEGIANCE: Republic
HOMEWORLD: Kamino

ABILITIES: Armed and unarmed combat, military tactics

All clone troopers are trained in the use of cold-weather gear, but cold assault troopers are routinely stationed on frigid worlds with tough conditions. These troopers wear HT-77 armor designed to keep them warm and use equipment to aid them in these environments.

RIOT TROOPER

SPECIES: Human (clone)
HEIGHT: 1.83 m (6 ft)
ALLEGIANCE: Republic
HOMEWORLD: Kamino

ABILITIES: Armed and unarmed combat, military tactics, security, tracking, reconnaissance

Riot troopers are specially trained members of the Coruscant Guard who control crowds through shows of authority and nonlethal weapons, such as stun batons. They await orders in Coruscant barracks and often assist police in keeping the peace and hunting down fugitives.

FLAMETROOPER

SPECIES: Human (clone)
HEIGHT: 1.83 m (6 ft)
ALLEGIANCE: Republic

HOMEWORLD: Kamino
ABILITIES: Armed and unarmed combat, heavy weaponry

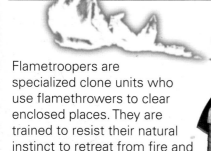

Flametroopers are specialized clone units who use flamethrowers to clear enclosed places. They are trained to resist their natural instinct to retreat from fire and rely on insulated body gloves, coolant reservoirs, and fireproof equipment to prevail in tackling dangerous objectives.

CLONE CADET

SPECIES: Human (clone)
HEIGHT: Varies
ALLEGIANCE: Republic
HOMEWORLD: Kamino

ABILITIES: Armed and unarmed combat, military tactics, heavy weaponry

Clone troopers grow to maturity in just a decade. They spend much of their accelerated childhoods in military training, learning tactics, and engaging in countless drills. Most of their education takes place on Kamino, but cadets also pursue offworld missions as part of Youth Brigades.

CLONE GUNNER

SPECIES: Human (clone)
HEIGHT: 1.83 m (6 ft)
ALLEGIANCE: Republic
HOMEWORLD: Kamino

ABILITIES: Armed and unarmed combat, military tactics, heavy weaponry

Clone gunners operate artillery installations and the turbolasers of starships, relying on specialized training to anticipate enemy tactics and target opponents effectively. They wear reinforced armor for protection against recoil from their guns and helmets insulated to reduce both noise and vibrations.

JET TROOPER

SPECIES: Human (clone)
HEIGHT: 1.83 m (6 ft)
ALLEGIANCE: Republic
HOMEWORLD: Kamino

ABILITIES: Armed and unarmed combat, military tactics, survival, starfighter/ starship piloting

Jet troopers are trained in aerial maneuvers and combat, using jetpacks to scout ahead of clone units and deny enemies the tactical advantage of the high ground. Jet troopers help defend the Republic on Cato Neimoidia and Anaxes and take part in the Battle of Yerbana in the final days of the Clone Wars.

SPECIAL OPS TROOPER

SPECIES: Human (clone)
HEIGHT: 1.83 m (6 ft)
ALLEGIANCE: Republic
HOMEWORLD: Kamino

ABILITIES: Armed and unarmed combat, military tactics, heavy weaponry

Special ops troopers act as the eyes and ears of other clone units, moving stealthily into position and gathering intelligence about potential enemies on the battlefield. Their specialized gear allows them to detect hazards at a distance. They prove invaluable in the Battle of Christophsis and the Second Battle of Geonosis.

STEALTH PILOT

SPECIES: Human (clone)
HEIGHT: 1.83 m (6 ft)
ALLEGIANCE: Republic
HOMEWORLD: Kamino

ABILITIES: Armed and unarmed combat, military tactics, heavy weaponry

Clone pilots chosen to fly experimental stealth ships, such as the IPV-2C, succeed in their missions by slipping through enemy lines without being detected. During the Battle of Christophsis, stealth pilots help Anakin Skywalker fly through a Separatist blockade, gathering data to be studied later.

SHEEV PALPATINE/DARTH SIDIOUS

REPUBLIC LEADER/HIDDEN SITH MASTER

Sheev Palpatine is the Supreme Chancellor of the Republic, working tirelessly to keep galactic civilization intact amid a devastating war. But this seemingly humble public servant has a secret identity. He is Darth Sidious, the hidden Sith Lord, and has engineered the Clone Wars to rule the galaxy.

A SENATOR'S RISE
Palpatine represented Naboo in the Senate a decade before the Clone Wars. When the Trade Federation invaded the planet, he advised Naboo's Queen Amidala as she begged the Senate for help. The Senate responded to her plea with pointless bickering, so Amidala called for a no-confidence vote in Chancellor Valorum. The Senate then voted to make Palpatine his replacement.

GROWING POWERS
As the war drags on, Palpatine is given more and more emergency powers to counter the Separatists' attacks. He has the support of the Senate's Loyalist faction, but over time Loyalists such as Bail Organa and Padmé Amidala begin to worry about the vast amount of power he's gathered. Palpatine vows to give up this power once the war has been won. But will he keep his promise?

As the Sith Lord Darth Sidious, Palpatine is a master of the dark side and controls both sides in the Clone Wars. He appears as the Republic's Chancellor while his apprentice, Count Dooku, leads the Separatists. As the war grinds on, Palpatine manipulates events so he gains more power as Chancellor, and those urging caution or peace are silenced or eliminated.

SPECIES: Human
HEIGHT: 1.73 m (5 ft 8 in)
ALLEGIANCE: Sith
HOMEWORLD: Naboo

ABILITIES: Force sensitivity, lightsaber combat, knowledge of Sith lore, Sith sorcery, manipulate events, leadership, diplomacy, political strategy

Cowl hides face from Sidious' agents

"ONE SHUDDERS TO THINK WHERE THE GALAXY WOULD BE WITHOUT THE JEDI."

– Palpatine

Dark-side power makes Sidious a deadly duelist

TIMELINE

82 BSW4	Born on Naboo
32 BSW4	Engineers Trade Federation invasion of Naboo
32 BSW4	Becomes Supreme Chancellor
22 BSW4	Granted wartime powers to combat Separatists
21 BSW4	Plots kidnap of Force-sensitive children to use as dark-side agents
20 BSW4	Ruins peace negotiations to ensure further production of clone troops
20 BSW4	Arranges Naboo assassination plot to manipulate Anakin Skywalker
19 BSW4	Foils Jedi investigation into clones' inhibitor chips
19 BSW4	Reveals true identity to Anakin and seduces him into becoming his new apprentice
19 BSW4	Issues Order 66, with clones obediently killing most of the galaxy's Jedi
19 BSW4	Declares Republic is now Galactic Empire, with Palpatine as its Emperor

DARK DESIGN

To rule the galaxy, Sidious must destroy the Jedi Order. At Chancellor Palpatine's urging, the Jedi reluctantly put aside their traditional role as peacekeepers to become generals leading the clone army. Many Jedi die in battle or lose faith, doubting whether the Order is doing the right thing. Meanwhile, the clone army has been created to support Sidious' master plan. Each clone has an inhibitor chip in his brain to ensure obedience to any command from Sidious. When Sidious issues Order 66, the clones target the Jedi, few of whom survive the attack.

COUNT DOOKU

FALLEN JEDI

Count Dooku is the Separatists' public leader and a former Jedi who lost faith in the Order and left its ranks. Most in the galaxy think Dooku is merely a politician and an opponent of the Republic. While the Jedi know that Dooku has fallen to the dark side and become a Sith, they do not know his Sith title, or if he is the master or the apprentice.

"THE SITH CONTROL EVERYTHING—YOU JUST DON'T KNOW IT."

– Count Dooku

A MASTER'S COMMANDS

General Grievous commands the Separatists' droid armies, with Dooku appearing as the breakaway government's political leader. But Dooku frequently clashes with the Jedi on missions for his master, Darth Sidious, fighting a series of duels with Obi-Wan Kenobi and Anakin Skywalker. He takes his own dark-side apprentice, Asajj Ventress, but eventually obeys his master's command to cast her aside.

Ventress survives and retreats to Dathomir, where she and a coven of dark-side witches known as the Nightsisters plot revenge. After an assassination attempt on Dooku's homeworld Serenno fails, the leader of the Nightsisters, Mother Talzin, sends Dooku a new apprentice, Savage Opress, whose secret mission is to kill him. Dooku survives this second plot against his life and vows to destroy the Nightsisters.

SPECIES: Human
HEIGHT: 1.93 m (6 ft 4 in)
ALLEGIANCE: Sith
HOMEWORLD: Serenno

ABILITIES: Force sensitivity, lightsaber combat, leadership, public speaking, military tactics

IDENTITY REVEALED

The Jedi discover the mysterious Tyranus recruited Jango Fett as source material for the clone army. When new clues arise about Jedi Master Sifo-Dyas' death, Sidious orders Dooku to tie up any loose ends that could reveal the truth about the clones' secret purpose to wipe out the Jedi. On Oba Diah, Anakin and Obi-Wan duel Dooku and discover he is Tyranus.

Lightsaber features unusual curved hilt

Belt made of rancor hide

TIMELINE

102 BSW4	Born into nobility and wealth on Serenno
102 BSW4	Enters Jedi Order
42 BSW4	Leaves Jedi, reclaiming title on Serenno
32 BSW4	Has Sifo-Dyas killed and assumes his identity to complete the original clone army order
32 BSW4	Recruits Jango Fett as prime clone for the army
24 BSW4	Appears as public leader of the Separatists
22 BSW4	Takes part in the First Battle of Geonosis
21 BSW4	Backs Death Watch's attempt to take over Mandalore
20 BSW4	Ordered by Darth Sidious to kill Asajj Ventress
20 BSW4	Orders General Grievous to destroy Nightsisters
19 BSW4	Battles Anakin and Obi-Wan on Oba Diah, and his identity as Tyranus is revealed
19 BSW4	Held captive by Mother Talzin and Maul on Dathomir, but saved by Sidious
19 BSW4	Takes part in kidnapping of Palpatine
19 BSW4	Defeated by Anakin and killed on Palpatine's orders

VOICE OF THE OPPOSITION

The Separatists broadcast Dooku's passionate, fiery speeches to Republic worlds. His charisma is a vital Separatist weapon in the fight for political advantage.

ASAJJ VENTRESS

DARK SIDE ASSASSIN

The fallen Jedi Padawan Asajj Ventress serves Count Dooku as an assassin, battling the Jedi on many missions during the Clone Wars. When Dooku rejects her as his apprentice and tries to kill her, Ventress seeks a new path, returning home to Dathomir before working as a bounty hunter. Asajj's life then takes a final, surprising turn.

SEARCHING FOR BELONGING

Ventress' life is filled with turmoil and a search for belonging. Born to the Nightsisters, the young Asajj is sold to a pirate who takes her to Rattatak, where she becomes Padawan to a stranded Jedi, Ky Narec. When Narec is killed, Ventress gives into her rage and takes over the planet. Dooku discovers her and recruits her as his agent but is forced to betray her on orders from his own Sith master, the mysterious Darth Sidious.

Asajj returns to Dathomir and is welcomed back by the Nightsisters' leader, Mother Talzin, who helps her try to kill Dooku. When their attempt fails, Asajj's sisters are wiped out by the Separatists, leaving her alone again.

"YOU HAVE YOUR OWN PATH TO FOLLOW NOW."

– Mother Talzin

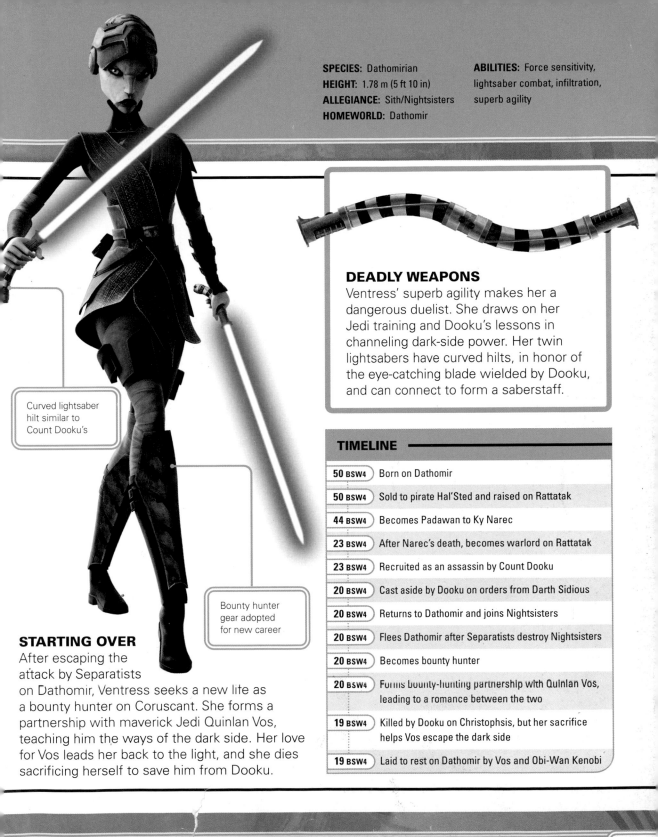

SPECIES: Dathomirian
HEIGHT: 1.78 m (5 ft 10 in)
ALLEGIANCE: Sith/Nightsisters
HOMEWORLD: Dathomir

ABILITIES: Force sensitivity, lightsaber combat, infiltration, superb agility

Curved lightsaber hilt similar to Count Dooku's

DEADLY WEAPONS

Ventress' superb agility makes her a dangerous duelist. She draws on her Jedi training and Dooku's lessons in channeling dark-side power. Her twin lightsabers have curved hilts, in honor of the eye-catching blade wielded by Dooku, and can connect to form a saberstaff.

Bounty hunter gear adopted for new career

STARTING OVER

After escaping the attack by Separatists on Dathomir, Ventress seeks a new life as a bounty hunter on Coruscant. She forms a partnership with maverick Jedi Quinlan Vos, teaching him the ways of the dark side. Her love for Vos leads her back to the light, and she dies sacrificing herself to save him from Dooku.

TIMELINE

50 BSW4	Born on Dathomir
50 BSW4	Sold to pirate Hal'Sted and raised on Rattatak
44 BSW4	Becomes Padawan to Ky Narec
23 BSW4	After Narec's death, becomes warlord on Rattatak
23 BSW4	Recruited as an assassin by Count Dooku
20 BSW4	Cast aside by Dooku on orders from Darth Sidious
20 BSW4	Returns to Dathomir and joins Nightsisters
20 BSW4	Flees Dathomir after Separatists destroy Nightsisters
20 BSW4	Becomes bounty hunter
20 BSW4	Forms bounty-hunting partnership with Quinlan Vos, leading to a romance between the two
19 BSW4	Killed by Dooku on Christophsis, but her sacrifice helps Vos escape the dark side
19 BSW4	Laid to rest on Dathomir by Vos and Obi-Wan Kenobi

Obi-Wan Kenobi cut Maul in two in a duel on Naboo, but the power of the dark side and Maul's own ferocious will preserved his life. Restored to strength and sanity, he seeks revenge against both the Jedi and Darth Sidious, building a galactic crime syndicate and seizing control of the planet Mandalore.

A BROTHER'S QUEST

Maul rose to power as Sidious' Sith apprentice. He killed Jedi Master Qui-Gon Jinn on Naboo but was felled in turn by Jedi Padawan Obi-Wan Kenobi. Maul survived but was left insane, trapped on junkyard planet Lotho Minor. His brother Savage Opress rescues him with the aid of Mother Talzin—their mother and leader of the Nightsister witches—who heals Maul's mind. With Savage's help, Maul plots to unite the galaxy's criminal gangs and strike back against everyone who wronged him.

Maul quickly gathers power, uniting Mandalore's Death Watch warriors with the Hutts, the Pykes, and Black Sun gangs to form the Shadow Collective. He kills the head of Death Watch, Pre Vizsla, and takes revenge on Obi-Wan by killing his beloved Duchess Satine Kryze, Mandalore's leader. Maul now rules, but his rise alarms Sidious. In a furious duel, Sidious kills Savage and defeats his former apprentice, imprisoning him on Stygeon Prime. But Maul will return to threaten the galaxy anew.

SPECIES: Dathomirian Zabrak
HEIGHT: 1.83 m (6 ft)
ALLEGIANCE: Shadow Collective
HOMEWORLD: Dathomir

ABILITIES: Force sensitivity, exceptional agility, lightsaber combat, unarmed combat, desire for revenge drives will to survive

All Zabraks have distinctive cranial horns

Double-bladed lightsaber of ancient Sith design

Replacement legs forged by Mother Talzin

NEW ORDER'S RISE

Maul is soon rescued by Death Watch, but he is unaware Sidious allowed this escape and is manipulating him so he can destroy Mother Talzin. Maul then returns to Mandalore, which is engulfed in a civil war between Death Watch and the Nite Owls resistance group. The Republic's clone troopers aid the Nite Owls, with Ahsoka Tano capturing Maul. But on Maul and Ahsoka's way to Coruscant, Order 66 causes the clones to attack them. A desperate Ahsoka frees Maul to cause chaos so she can escape. Maul flees but is already plotting to rebuild his criminal empire.

TIMELINE

32 BSW4	Kills Qui-Gon on Naboo, cut down by Obi-Wan
32 BSW4	Exiled on junkyard world of Lotho Minor
20 BSW4	Found by Savage Opress, Mother Talzin restores Maul's mind and crafts mechanical legs for him
20 BSW4	Duels Obi-Wan on Raydonia
19 BSW4	Rises to leadership of Shadow Collective
19 BSW4	Kills Pre Vizsla and Duchess Satine Kryze, becomes ruler of Mandalore
19 BSW4	Defeated by Sidious and temporarily imprisoned
19 BSW4	Escapes Dathomir after death of Mother Talzin
19 BSW4	Adds Crimson Dawn to Shadow Collective's ranks
19 BSW4	Siege of Mandalore ends with Maul captured by Republic clone troopers
19 BSW4	Escapes Republic custody during Order 66

"YOU CANNOT IMAGINE THE DEPTHS I WOULD GO TO ... TO STAY ALIVE."

– Maul

MOTHER TALZIN

NIGHTSISTER SHAMAN

Robes of Nightsister shaman

SPECIES: Dathomirian
HEIGHT: 2.23 m (7 ft 4 in)
ALLEGIANCE: Nightsisters
HOMEWORLD: Dathomir

ABILITIES: Force magic, leadership, spiritual guidance, clairvoyance, foreknowledge, telekinesis

Mother Talzin is the spiritual leader of the Nightsisters of Dathomir. This powerful sorceress commands strange magicks based on Force lore unknown to the Jedi or Sith and sells her clan's services to any who can meet her price. Talzin longs to take revenge on Darth Sidious, who promised her a place at his side—but instead stole her son Maul to be his Sith apprentice.

"WHERE ONE SEES FAILURE, OTHERS SEE OPPORTUNITY."

– Mother Talzin

SHOWDOWN WITH SIDIOUS

Talzin welcomes Asajj Ventress back to the Nightsisters after Count Dooku betrays her. She then helps Asajj and Savage Opress plot to destroy him. However, the plan fails, and General Grievous wipes out the Nightsisters. Talzin escapes, but Sidious corners her on Dathomir, and Grievous ends her life.

SAVAGE OPRESS

MONSTROUS CREATION

SPECIES: Dathomirian Zabrak
HEIGHT: 2.18 m (7 ft 2 in)
ALLEGIANCE: Nightsisters
HOMEWORLD: Dathomir

ABILITIES: Force sensitivity, lightsaber combat, immense physical strength

Mother Talzin's spells transform her son Savage Opress into a huge warrior, and she sends him to Count Dooku as a new apprentice. But Savage remains loyal to Talzin, and his true goal is to kill Dooku. He fails and begins a new quest: to find his lost brother Maul. Opress then becomes Maul's enforcer in the Shadow Collective.

PAWN OF DARKNESS
Savage agrees to serve Asajj Ventress to save his younger brother Feral's life. Talzin's magicks swell Savage's muscles and rage. Despite previously saving his brother's life, Opress kills Feral as a test of loyalty to Asajj. After being used as a pawn in so many plots, he is mortally wounded by Darth Sidious. As Savage dies, Talzin's spells fade; his anger ebbs, and his ruined body shrinks to its natural size.

"I'M NOT LIKE YOU. I NEVER WAS."
— Savage Opress to Maul

Body swollen by Nightsister sorcery

Dooku trains Savage to use a twin-bladed saber

FERAL

SPECIES: Dathomirian Zabrak
HEIGHT: 1.86 m (6 ft 1 in)
ALLEGIANCE: Nightbrothers
HOMEWORLD: Dathomir
ABILITIES: Martial arts, agility

Feral is one of Savage Opress' brothers. He competes in the tournament arranged for Asajj Ventress to select a warrior for her plan to kill Count Dooku. Savage saves Feral's life by promising to serve Ventress but then murders Feral as a test of loyalty to Asajj.

BROTHER VISCUS

SPECIES: Dathomirian Zabrak
HEIGHT: 1.88 m (6 ft 2 in)
ALLEGIANCE: Nightbrothers
HOMEWORLD: Dathomir
ABILITIES: Martial arts, military tactics, leadership

Viscus is the leader of the Nightbrothers on Dathomir, and he arranges the tournament in which Asajj Ventress selects Savage Opress to serve her. Viscus and several Nightbrothers later help Maul battle Count Dooku and General Grievous on Ord Mantell. He is badly wounded but manages to survive.

OLD DAKA

SPECIES: Dathomirian
HEIGHT: 1.83 m (6 ft)
ALLEGIANCE: Nightsisters
HOMEWORLD: Dathomir
ABILITIES: Force magic, leadership, spiritual guidance, clairvoyance, foreknowledge

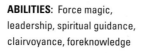

Old Daka is a Nightsister matriarch with a mastery of powerful, ancient Force sorcery. When General Grievous attacks Dathomir with a droid army, Mother Talzin requests Daka's help, and she reanimates dead Nightsisters to fight alongside the living. Grievous tracks her down and ends her long life.

ZOMBIE NIGHTSISTERS

SPECIES: Dathomirian (zombie)
HEIGHT: Varies
ALLEGIANCE: Nightsisters
HOMEWORLD: Dathomir
ABILITIES: Unarmed combat

After their deaths, Dathomir's Nightsisters are shrouded in cocoons that hang from the planet's trees. When the Separatists attack the Nightsisters, Old Daka uses ancient magic to reanimate the dead. They emerge from their cocoons and overwhelm the droid invaders until Daka's death ends the spell.

KARIS

SPECIES: Dathomirian
HEIGHT: 1.9 m (6 ft 3 in)
ALLEGIANCE: Nightsisters
HOMEWORLD: Dathomir

ABILITIES: Armed and unarmed combat, agility, Force sensitivity, infiltration

Karis and her sister Naa'leth are two of the Nightsisters' best warriors. They join Asajj Ventress for a raid on Serenno with Count Dooku as their target, but Ventress' former master proves to be a tougher opponent than they had imagined. Karis returns to Dathomir and dies battling General Grievous' droid armies.

TALIA

SPECIES: Dathomirian
HEIGHT: 1.85 m (6 ft 1 in)
ALLEGIANCE: Nightsisters
HOMEWORLD: Dathomir

ABILITIES: Armed and unarmed combat, agility, Force sensitivity

Talia is a Nightsister who assists Mother Talzin on many missions, from preparing the spells that heal Asajj Ventress to presenting the warrior Savage Opress to Count Dooku on Serenno. Like nearly all of her clan, Talia falls fighting General Grievous and his army of battle droids.

NAA'LETH

SPECIES: Dathomirian
HEIGHT: 1.85 m (6 ft 1 in)
ALLEGIANCE: Nightsisters
HOMEWORLD: Dathomir

ABILITIES: Armed and unarmed combat, agility, Force sensitivity, infiltration

Naa'leth is sister to Karis and considered one of the Nightsisters' greatest fighters. She joins Asajj Ventress on the raid on Count Dooku's stronghold, then returns there when Mother Talzin brings Savage Opress to Dooku as a servant. She dies defending her clan from Separatist invaders.

LUCE

SPECIES: Dathomirian
HEIGHT: 2 m (6 ft 7 in)
ALLEGIANCE: Nightsisters
HOMEWORLD: Dathomir

ABILITIES: Armed and unarmed combat, agility, Force sensitivity

Luce is an accomplished warrior of the Nightsister clan living on Dathomir. She helps defend Mother Talzin and her sisters against an army of battle droids led by General Grievous, taking many invaders down with an energy bow and blaster rifles. Mortally wounded in the fight, she urges Asajj Ventress to save herself.

GENERAL GRIEVOUS

CYBORG WARLORD

General Grievous is the Separatists' military commander, whose name strikes terror in citizens of Republic worlds. He has replaced much of his living body with mechanical parts, voluntarily making himself into a cybernetic warrior with enormous strength, power, and speed. Grievous hates the Jedi and takes the lightsabers of those he kills as trophies.

WAR MACHINE
Grievous learned the art of lightsaber combat from Count Dooku and can wield four laser swords at once. He uses his mechanical arms to rotate his lightsabers so rapidly that they become pinwheels of destructive energy. While Grievous has no Force ability, his artificial limbs and cybernetic systems give him reflexes and

agility to rival those of the Jedi Knights. He takes macabre delight in beating Jedi on the battlefield. When up against an enemy he can't handle, he is quick to turn tail and run, often scuttling away to safety using all four limbs.

A WARLORD'S IMPROVEMENTS
Very little of Grievous' original Kaleesh body remains, but the Separatist warlord insists his radical transformation was his own choice, calling his artificial abilities "improvements."

"I DO NOT CARE ABOUT YOUR POLITICS. I DO NOT CARE ABOUT YOUR REPUBLIC. I ONLY LIVE TO SEE YOU DIE!"

– General Grievous

SPECIES: Kaleesh (cyborg)
HEIGHT: 2.16 m (7 ft 1 in)
ALLEGIANCE: Separatists
HOMEWORLD: Kalee

ABILITIES: Lightsaber combat, superb reflexes and agility, starship piloting, military tactics

TIMELINE

22 BSW4	Commands *Malevolence* in attack on Republic at Abregado
22 BSW4	Duels Ahsoka Tano on Skytop Station
21 BSW4	Kills Nahdar Vebb on Vassek 3, retreats from Kit Fisto
21 BSW4	Captures Eeth Koth at Saleucami and duels with Obi-Wan Kenobi
21 BSW4	Leads Separatist assault on Kamino
20 BSW4	Captured by Republic on Naboo, but released in exchange for Anakin
20 BSW4	Wipes out Nightsisters
19 BSW4	Battles Maul and Shadow Collective on Zanbar
19 BSW4	Bombards Ord Mantell and is briefly captured
19 BSW4	Kills Mother Talzin on Dathomir
19 BSW4	Leads raid on Coruscant, briefly capturing Supreme Chancellor Palpatine
19 BSW4	Becomes Separatist leader after death of Dooku
19 BSW4	Killed by Obi-Wan on Utapau

Magnetized talons of durasteel

He hates droids and flies into a destructive rage if anyone is foolish enough to mistake him for a mechanical creation.

APPETITE FOR DESTRUCTION

Grievous leads Separatist fleets that conquer Republic worlds and leave them burned and broken. The Republic destroys his mightiest flagship, the *Malevolence*, at the Dead Moon of Antar, but Grievous escapes to fight on.

He clashes with the Jedi, fighting battles with Obi-Wan Kenobi, Ahsoka Tano, Eeth Koth, and Adi Gallia. In the final days of the war, he leads a daring raid on Coruscant to kidnap Supreme Chancellor Palpatine. He escapes again, but Obi-Wan tracks him down and destroys him on Utapau.

NUTE GUNRAY

SPECIES: Neimoidian
HEIGHT: 1.91 m (6 ft 3 in)
ALLEGIANCE: Separatists
HOMEWORLD: Neimoidia

ABILITIES: Leadership, negotiations, escaping justice

As viceroy of the Trade Federation, Nute Gunray was manipulated into invading Naboo, a crisis that set the stage for the Clone Wars. Republic courts put him on trial four times, but Gunray always escaped justice and managed to keep his titles and wealth. The viceroy then became a key leader of Count Dooku's Separatist Alliance.

Gunray burns for revenge against Padmé Amidala, whom he blames for his humiliating defeat on Naboo. He forces Rodia's senator, Onaconda Farr, into capturing Padmé and is arrested when his plot collapses. But Gunray escapes again, with help from Asajj Ventress.

Ornate headdress is a sign of wealth

POGGLE THE LESSER

SPECIES: Geonosian
HEIGHT: 1.83 m (6 ft)
ALLEGIANCE: Separatists
HOMEWORLD: Geonosis

ABILITIES: Leadership, military tactics, engineering, negotiations

Staff of Command is symbol of office

Poggle the Lesser is Archduke of Geonosis and an important Separatist leader. Geonosian hive-foundries turn out endless battle droids and vehicles for Count Dooku's armies and research terrifying superweapons as well. Poggle hates the Republic and defies every effort to bring Geonosis to heel.

The Republic captures Poggle after the Second Battle of Geonosis, interrogating him and forcing him to work on its weapons projects. But his loyalties never waver, and he soon escapes and goes back to working to help the Separatists prevail in the war.

GENERAL KALANI

MODEL: ST-series military strategic analysis and tactics droid
HEIGHT: 1.94 m (6 ft 4 in)
ALLEGIANCE: Separatists

MANUFACTURER: Baktoid Combat Automata
ABILITIES: Armor, leadership, enhanced strategic programming, resistance to interrogation

General Kalani is a super tactical droid who leads Separatist efforts to crush the resistance on Onderon. The task is assigned to him by Count Dooku after the puppet monarch Sanjay Rash fails. Kalani ruthlessly pursues this goal, but his attempts to stamp out rebellion only make the opposition bolder.

Kalani proves both arrogant and brutal as a commander, interrogating the rebel leader Saw Gerrera and supervising the attempted execution of Onderon's previous ruler. With the fight lost, he kills King Rash on Dooku's orders and retreats to Agamar.

Gear typical of Onderon resistance fighters

Powerful servomotors drive droid limbs

LUX BONTERI

SPECIES: Human
HEIGHT: 1.78 m (5 ft 10 in)
ALLEGIANCE: Separatists/Republic

HOMEWORLD: Onderon
ABILITIES: Leadership, diplomacy, armed and unarmed combat

Lux Bonteri is the son of Mina Bonteri, a senator in the Confederacy of Independent Systems. He begins the Clone Wars as a Separatist supporter, but after Count Dooku orders the assassination of his mother, Lux briefly allies himself with Death Watch's Mandalorian thugs, in hopes of avenging her death by eliminating Dooku.

Ahsoka Tano helps Lux see he's made a mistake, and he renounces his former allegiance. During the Separatist occupation of his homeworld, Onderon, Lux joins the resistance, helping free the planet. He then represents it in the Republic Senate, completing a difficult personal journey.

ADMIRAL TRENCH

SPECIES: Harch
HEIGHT: 1.89 m (6 ft 2 in)
ALLEGIANCE: Separatists

HOMEWORLD: Secundus Ando
ABILITIES: Military tactics, leadership

Admiral Trench is a legendary tactician, whose presence strikes fear in Republic officers familiar with his ruthlessness. The tough Harch survives his flagship's destruction at Christophsis, though half his body is replaced with cybernetic parts. Anakin Skywalker strikes Trench down at the Battle of Anaxes, ending his fabled career once and for all.

Pointer doubles as swagger stick

"I SMELL FEAR, AND IT SMELLS GOOD."

— Admiral Trench

LOK DURD

SPECIES: Neimoidian
HEIGHT: 2.11 m (6 ft 11 in)
ALLEGIANCE: Separatists

HOMEWORLD: Neimoidia
ABILITIES: Weapons research, leadership, tactics

Lok Durd is a Neimoidian weapons designer serving Count Dooku. He hopes his creations will help win the war and bring him wealth and glory. Durd tests the Defoliator tank, which destroys organic matter but leaves droids unharmed, on Maridun. The test succeeds, but Durd is captured by a party of Jedi refugees and their Lurmen allies.

MAR TUUK

SPECIES: Neimoidian
HEIGHT: 2.09 m (6 ft 10 in)
ALLEGIANCE: Separatists

HOMEWORLD: Neimoidia
ABILITIES: Military tactics, battlefield leadership, evasion

The veteran naval officer Mar Tuuk is a shrewd tactician, who leads the Separatist blockade of Ryloth. He is certain he can predict Anakin Skywalker's moves and maintain the blockade. Anakin bests Tuuk by being unpredictable, flying a ruined cruiser on a daring solo mission and forcing Tuuk to abandon ship.

RIFF TAMSON

SPECIES: Karkarodon
HEIGHT: 2.21 m (7 ft 3 in)
ALLEGIANCE: Separatists
HOMEWORLD: Karkaris

ABILITIES: Military tactics, intimidation, diplomacy, persuasion, crushing bite

Riff Tamson is a sharklike Karkarodon, who incites a civil war between the planet Mon Cala's Quarren and Mon Calamari peoples. He then invades the aquatic world with Separatist droids. A ruthless commander, Tamson is also deadly in combat, attacking with his powerful jaws and sharp teeth. He is killed in battle by Mon Cala's young Prince Lee-Char.

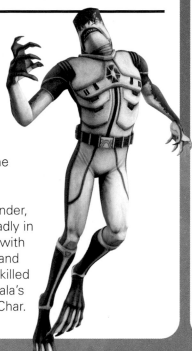

WHORM LOATHSOM

SPECIES: Kerkoiden
HEIGHT: 1.75 m (5 ft 9 in)
ALLEGIANCE: Separatists

HOMEWORLD: Kerkoidia
ABILITIES: Military tactics, diplomacy

Whorm Loathsom commands the armies of the Retail Caucus, an organization loyal to the Separatists. He is sent to seize the key world of Christophsis. Loathsom makes a critical error by letting Obi-Wan drag out negotiations, allowing the Republic to regroup and repel the Separatist assault.

WAT TAMBOR

SPECIES: Skakoan
HEIGHT: 1.98 m (6 ft 6 in)
ALLEGIANCE: Separatists
HOMEWORLD: Skako

ABILITIES: Engineering, logistics, leadership

The foreman of the wealthy Techno Union, Wat Tambor is one of the earliest backers of the Separatist Alliance. He requires a protective suit to survive away from the high pressure of Skako's atmosphere. Tambor oversees the cruel occupation of Ryloth until the planet is liberated. On Skako Minor, he later performs experiments on the captured ARC trooper Echo to turn him into a tool to predict Republic tactics.

Vocabulator processes Skakoan speech

KARINA THE GREAT

SPECIES: Geonosian (queen)
HEIGHT: 8.6 m (28 ft 3 in)
ALLEGIANCE: Geonosians
HOMEWORLD: Geonosis

ABILITIES: Strength, drone servants, leadership, intimidation

Karina the Great is the secret queen of the Stalgasin Geonosian hive, who gives orders to Poggle the Lesser from a secret lair. There, Karina lays eggs and controls an army of drones and undead Geonosians reanimated by brain worms. Her attempt to use the worms to control Jedi minds fails, and she is buried in the wreckage of her secret stronghold.

OSI SOBECK

SPECIES: Phindian
HEIGHT: 2.03 m (6 ft 8 in)
ALLEGIANCE: Separatists
HOMEWORLD: Phindar

ABILITIES: Military tactics, leadership, interrogation, armed and unarmed combat

Osi Sobeck is the warden of the Separatist prison known as the Citadel. After Jedi Master Even Piell and Captain Tarkin's capture, he interrogates them to learn the coordinates of a secret hyperlane, the Nexus Route. Both prisoners resist his brutal methods, and Sobeck dies battling the Jedi and clones sent to retrieve the pair and the secret they have protected.

KRAKEN

MODEL: ST-series military strategic analysis and tactics droid
HEIGHT: 1.94 m (6 ft 4 in)
ALLEGIANCE: Separatists

MANUFACTURER: Baktoid Combat Automata
ABILITIES: Armor, leadership, enhanced strategic programming, resistance to interrogation

Kraken serves under Admiral Trench during the Battle of Ringo Vinda and is told to bring Tup, a captive clone trooper, to Serenno to stop the Republic from studying his malfunctioning inhibitor chip. Anakin Skywalker strikes off the super tactical droid's head and arms, but Kraken is rebuilt and resumes his Separatist service, taking command of a fleet blockading Scipio.

MINA BONTERI

Elegant Onderonian dress

SPECIES: Human
HEIGHT: 1.78 m (5 ft 10 in)
ALLEGIANCE: Separatists
HOMEWORLD: Onderon

ABILITIES: Legislative strategy, diplomacy, leadership, persuasion

Mina Bonteri is a Separatist senator who was a mentor for Padmé Amidala before Mina left the Republic. Despite their political differences, Padmé secretly meets Bonteri in the Raxus system in hopes of finding a peaceful end to the war. When their efforts gain momentum, Count Dooku orders Bonteri's assassination. Her orphaned son Lux vows to avenge his mother by eliminating Count Dooku.

NUVO VINDI

SPECIES: Faust
HEIGHT: 2.07 m (6 ft 9 in)
ALLEGIANCE: Separatists
HOMEWORLD: Adana

ABILITIES: Scientific knowledge, genetic engineering

Nuvo Vindi is a Faust scientist who works in a secret lab hidden in the swamplands of Naboo. The Separatists hope Vindi can create a virus that targets clone troopers, but he secretly pursues a terrifying dream: to recreate the deadly Blue Shadow Virus and release it, which would wipe the Galaxy clean of life. Fortunately for both the Republic and the Separatists, Vindi's terrible plan is thwarted.

LEP-86C8

MODEL: LEP-series service droid
HEIGHT: 1.26 m (4 ft 2 in)
ALLEGIANCE: None

MANUFACTURER: Coachelle Automata
ABILITIES: Service tasks

LEP servant droids act as assistants and valets, faithfully performing errands for their masters. LEP-86C8 serves Nuvo Vindi in his Naboo lab and is entrusted with a bomb that contains a vial of the Blue Shadow Virus. Padmé Amidala, Ahsoka Tano, and a clone-trooper squad hunt desperately for Vindi's loyal little droid, all too aware that the fate of the Galaxy may hang in the balance.

R3-S6

MODEL: R-series astromech droid
HEIGHT: 1.09 m (3 ft 7 in)
ALLEGIANCE: Separatists
MANUFACTURER: Industrial Automaton

ABILITIES: Starship maintenance, information retrieval, repairs, starfighter piloting

R3-S6, known as Goldie, is assigned to Anakin Skywalker after R2-D2 is lost at the Battle of Bothawui. The droid tries Anakin's patience with his many mistakes and is revealed as an enemy agent reporting to General Grievous. R2-D2 destroys Goldie in a duel at Skytop Station.

A-4D

MODEL: A4 laboratory assistant droid
HEIGHT: 1.74 m (5 ft 9 in)
ALLEGIANCE: Separatists

MANUFACTURER: MerenData
ABILITIES: Surgery, medical procedures, diagnostics, supervisor protocols

A-4D is a versatile surgical droid who repairs General Grievous' cybernetic systems after his battles with Jedi and clones. He has a sarcastic streak and talks more than Grievous likes, but the droid is both loyal and useful. Kit Fisto dismantles A-4D with his lightsaber, but Grievous quickly has his invaluable servant rebuilt.

CAPTAIN ARGYUS

SPECIES: Human
HEIGHT: 1.83 m (6 ft)
ALLEGIANCE: Separatists
HOMEWORLD: Tepasi

ABILITIES: Armed and unarmed combat, military tactics, security

Faro Argyus is the fifth generation of his family to serve in the Senate Guard, but he betrays his oath to the Republic and joins the Separatist cause. He helps Asajj Ventress free Nute Gunray from a Republic warship, fighting his way past Commander Gree and clone guards. But he never gets his reward, as Ventress ends his life with a thrust of her lightsaber.

SLICK

SPECIES: Human (clone)
HEIGHT: 1.83 m (6 ft)
ALLEGIANCE: Separatists
HOMEWORLD: Kamino

ABILITIES: Armed and unarmed combat, military tactics, leadership, infiltration

Slick is a sergeant in the clone army who concludes that the clones are little more than enslaved warriors for the Jedi and the Republic. During the fight for Christophsis, he provides intelligence to Asajj Ventress. His treachery is discovered by Captain Rex and Commander Cody, who apprehend him.

BEC LAWISE

SPECIES: Siniteen
HEIGHT: 1.74 m (5 ft 9 in)
ALLEGIANCE: Separatists
HOMEWORLD: Mileva

ABILITIES: Leadership, legislative strategy

Bec Lawise is a veteran politician who is the Speaker of the Separatist Senate. He still has many friends in the Republic and attends a peace conference on Mandalore, as well as joining the Separatist delegation to Scipio. He opposes Count Dooku's plot to seize control of the banks, a principled stance that costs him his life.

NOSSOR RI

SPECIES: Quarren
HEIGHT: 1.92 m (6 ft 4 in)
ALLEGIANCE: Separatists
HOMEWORLD: Mon Cala

ABILITIES: Leadership, negotiations

Nossor Ri is a Quarren leader on Mon Cala, a planet the Quarren share with the Mon Calamari. Fearing Prince Lee-Char is too inexperienced to rule, he joins forces with Riff Tamson and the Separatists to oppose him. But Ri soon realizes his mistake and helps the Mon Calamari and Republic forces fight against Tamson.

RISH LOO

SPECIES: Gungan
HEIGHT: 2.07 m (6 ft 9 in)
ALLEGIANCE: Separatists
HOMEWORLD: Naboo

ABILITIES: Persuasion, hypnosis, Gungan sorcery

Rish Loo is a Gungan priest and a member of the Gungan High Council. He uses sorcery to hypnotize Boss Lyonie into planning an attack on Naboo's capital, Thccd, in alliance with the Separatists. After this plan is thwarted by Anakin Skywalker, Padmé Amidala, and Jar Jar Binks, Count Dooku kills Loo for his failure.

KING SANJAY RASH

SPECIES: Human
HEIGHT: 1.74 m (5 ft 9 in)
ALLEGIANCE: Separatists
HOMEWORLD: Onderon

ABILITIES: Leadership, negotiations

Sanjay Rash schemes his way to the throne of Onderon, overthrowing King Ramsis Dendup, then breaks Dendup's vow of neutrality in the Clone Wars to become an ally of the Separatists. After Rash and General Kalani are defeated by rebel forces, Count Dooku gives up the fight, telling Kalani to do away with the puppet king and retreat.

BATTLE DROID

SEPARATIST SOLDIERS

B1 battle droids are simple, sturdy machines built by the billions in Separatist foundries and sent to invade planets loyal to the Republic. Clone troopers call the droids "clankers" and "tinnies," boasting that they're each worth 100 of them. But Separatist leaders can simply order more legions of B1s, and many clones have died fighting these foes.

IN THEIR MAKERS' IMAGE

The Geonosians designed battle droids to mimic their own insect-like bodies. Their first client was the Trade Federation, which used B1s to invade Naboo. That generation of B1s lacked independent programming, following orders from orbiting Control Ships. Later models can think for themselves but not particularly well: situations not encoded in their logic modules baffle them, allowing clone troopers to blast the flummoxed droids into scrap.

B1s can be reprogrammed—two B1s serve R2-D2 on a mission to free Jedi Master Even Piell from Lola Sayu. But pushing them beyond their standard programming risks malfunctions and poor performance. Battle droids assigned new duties often chatter endlessly about what they're doing, to the annoyance of Separatist commanders. This is a behavioral quirk caused by logic modules strained beyond their factory capabilities.

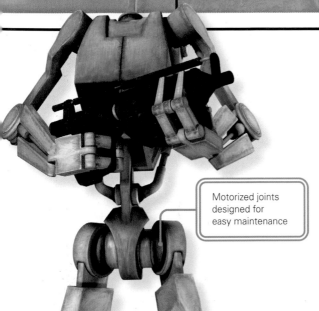

Antenna picks up remote commands

MODEL: Battle droid
HEIGHT: 1.91 m (6 ft 3 in)
ALLEGIANCE: Separatists
MANUFACTURER: Baktoid Armor Workshop

ABILITIES: Combat programming, crowd control, controlled remotely

NUMBERS GAME

Yes, B1s are lousy fighters: they are tactically inept, inaccurate with blasters, and easy to scrap. But they were designed to be cheap and disposable, overwhelming opposition through sheer numbers. This simple but effective plan has led to the conquest of many worlds by armies of "tinnies."

Motorized joints designed for easy maintenance

E-5 BLASTER RIFLE

Battle droids' standard armament is the E-5 blaster rifle, built by the Baktoid Armor Workshop. E-5s generate massive amounts of waste heat, which is no problem for droids but uncomfortable for living beings.

"ROGER ROGER."

– Battle droid

BATTLE DROID COMMANDER

MODEL: B1-series battle droid
HEIGHT: 1.93 m (6 ft 4 in)
ALLEGIANCE: Separatists
MANUFACTURER: Baktoid Combat Automata
ABILITIES: Combat, leadership

Battle droid commanders are variants of the B1 model with improved processors and superior programming. They take charge of other battle droids and can be distinguished from them by the yellow flares on their heads and chests. They enjoy bossing around regular B1s but quickly look for help from tactical droids or organic officers when things go poorly in battle.

BATTLE DROID PILOT

MODEL: B1-series battle droid
HEIGHT: 1.93 m (6 ft 4 in)
ALLEGIANCE: Separatists
MANUFACTURER: Baktoid Combat Automata
ABILITIES: Combat programming, piloting skills

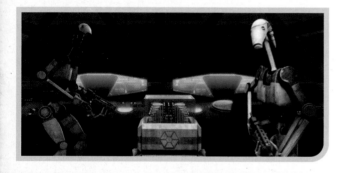

Battle droid pilots are nearly identical to standard B1 units, but they have beefed-up processors and programming that allow them to pilot ships and vehicles. Pilot droids also serve as bridge crews and are sometimes pressed into service as gunners and infantry, though they often protest such duty. Blue markings distinguish pilots from regular B1s.

SECURITY BATTLE DROID

MODEL: B1-series battle droid
HEIGHT: 1.93 m (6 ft 4 in)
ALLEGIANCE: Separatists
MANUFACTURER: Baktoid Combat Automata
ABILITIES: Combat programming, crowd control, sensor subroutines

B1 battle droids assigned to security sport red flares on their armor. These droids are often used as guards and sentries and are programmed to scan their surroundings for anything out of the ordinary. However, this often strains their logic modules, and security droids quickly become paranoid if not given regular memory wipes.

ROCKET BATTLE DROID

MODEL: B1-series battle droid
HEIGHT: 1.93 m (6 ft 4 in)
ALLEGIANCE: Separatists

MANUFACTURER: Baktoid Combat Automata
ABILITIES: Combat programming, aerial maneuvers

Jetpack is hardwired into B1's back

Rocket battle droids are standard B1s outfitted with jetpacks that let them maneuver in space. They have head-mounted lamps and laser cutters built into their arms. Rocket battle droids are dispatched from the massive Separatist battleship known as the *Malevolence* to hunt Plo Koon and his Wolfpack, a task they pursue with chilling enthusiasm.

FIREFIGHTER DROID

MODEL: B1-series battle droid
HEIGHT: 1.93 m (6 ft 4 in)
ALLEGIANCE: Separatists

MANUFACTURER: Baktoid Combat Automata
ABILITIES: Combat programming, firefighting ability

Firefighter droids are regular B1s remodeled to be effective at fighting fires within Separatist warships and installations. Specialized programming helps them respond to emergencies, while altered backpacks hold firefighting gear. They are adorned with yellow stripes and red flares to make them more visible in smoky conditions.

Hose can emit pressurized foam

AAT DRIVER DROID

MODEL: B1-series battle droid
HEIGHT: 1.93 m (6 ft 4 in)
ALLEGIANCE: Separatists

MANUFACTURER: Baktoid Combat Automata
ABILITIES: Combat programming, vehicle piloting

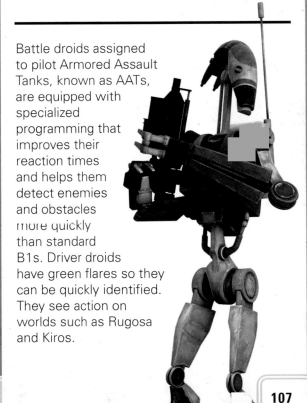

Battle droids assigned to pilot Armored Assault Tanks, known as AATs, are equipped with specialized programming that improves their reaction times and helps them detect enemies and obstacles more quickly than standard B1s. Driver droids have green flares so they can be quickly identified. They see action on worlds such as Rugosa and Kiros.

DESTROYER DROID

ROLLING DEATH

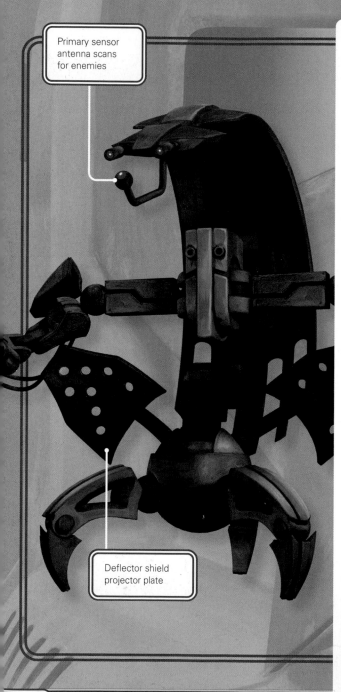

Primary sensor antenna scans for enemies

Deflector shield projector plate

MODEL: Destroyer droid
HEIGHT: 1.83 m (6 ft)
ALLEGIANCE: Separatists
MANUFACTURER: Colicoid Creation Nest

ABILITIES: Twin blaster cannons, shield projector, exceptional speed

Destroyer droids, often called droidekas or "rollies," are some of the toughest units in the Separatist arsenal. Destroyers roll into combat with terrifying speed, uncurl to snap onto their tripod legs, activate powerful defensive shield projectors, and start pumping blaster fire at their enemies. Clever and precise tactics are necessary to defeat them.

> **"THE TRICK IS TO GET THE RIGHT SPEED ON THE DROID POPPER."**
> – Ahsoka Tano

THE BEST DEFENSE
Ahsoka Tano teaches Onderon's rebels how to stop droidekas: the droids have a blind spot to their rear, and slow-moving objects will penetrate their shields. The trick is to work in pairs: one rebel attracts the destroyer's attention, while the other rolls an EMP grenade through its shield from behind.

SUPER BATTLE DROID

MECHANICAL MUSCLE

MODEL: B2-series super battle droid
HEIGHT: 1.93 m (6 ft 4 in)
ALLEGIANCE: Separatists

MANUFACTURER: Baktoid Combat Automata
ABILITIES: Heavy weapons, thick armor, aggressive programming

Super battle droids are the muscle of the Separatist infantry, built and programmed to be big and tough. Thick armor makes them hard to stop in combat, and their simple programming is all about aggression. These droids stomp straight at their enemies, sometimes shoving other battle droids aside in their haste to attack. Some B1s address their burly cousins as "sir" or "boss."

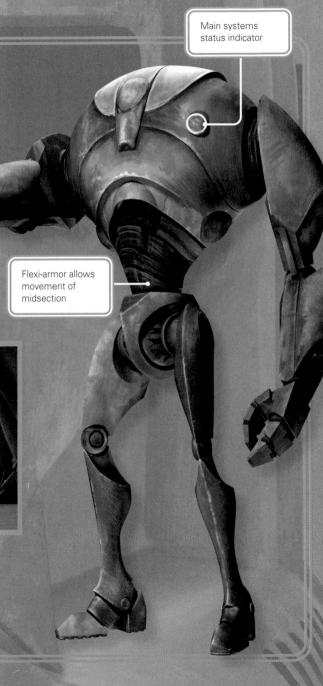

Main systems status indicator

Flexi-armor allows movement of midsection

DANGEROUS FOES

Wise clone troopers avoid taking on B2s directly, preferring to ambush them with EMP grenades, known as "droid poppers." These weapons generate electromagnetic pulses that cause the droids' systems to freeze. While the mighty machines are rebooting, clone units hurry to destroy them.

B2-HA SUPER BATTLE DROID

MODEL: B2-series super battle droid
HEIGHT: 1.93 m (6 ft 4 in)
ALLEGIANCE: Separatists

MANUFACTURER: Baktoid Combat Automata
ABILITIES: Heavy weapons, thick armor, aggressive programming, artillery

B2-HA Super Battle Droids are more powerful variants of the B2 with one arm sporting a warhead or torpedo launcher instead of the standard built-in laser cannon. They are sometimes given command of other battle droids, despite not being programmed for tactics or leadership.

B2-RP SUPER BATTLE DROID

MODEL: B2-series super battle droid
HEIGHT: 1.93 m (6 ft 4 in)
ALLEGIANCE: Separatists

MANUFACTURER: Baktoid Combat Automata
ABILITIES: Heavy weapons, thick armor, aggressive programming, flight

B2-RP Super Battle Droids augment the powerful weaponry of normal B2s with a built-in jetpack, creating a formidable aerial threat that Republic ground troops, fighters, and gunships must deal with. B2-RPs play a key role in the Separatist victory at Quell, boarding the damaged Star Destroyer *Liberty*.

B2 SUPER ROCKET TROOPER

MODEL: B2-series super battle droid
HEIGHT: 1.93 m (6 ft 4 in)
ALLEGIANCE: Separatists

MANUFACTURER: Baktoid Combat Automata
ABILITIES: Heavy weapons, thick armor, aggressive programming, improved flight

The Techno Union's military labs tinker with designs in search of an edge on the battlefield. One of their innovations is the B2 rocket trooper, an advance over the B2-RP model. These new droids are more maneuverable than their predecessors thanks to shoulder-mounted jetpacks and auxiliary boosters on their ankles.

SNIPER DROIDEKA

MODEL: Destroyer droid
HEIGHT: 1.87 m (6 ft 2 in)
ALLEGIANCE: Separatists
MANUFACTURER: Colicoid Creation Nest

ABILITIES: Combat programming, sniper programming, shield projectors, exceptional speed

Sniper droidekas are a variant model designed for sharpshooting. They are armed with a long-barreled blaster with tremendous range and power. However, they lack the standard droideka's shields, which would interfere with their long-range targeting.

GEONOSIAN DRONE

SPECIES: Geonosian
HEIGHT: 1.7 m (5 ft 7 in)
ALLEGIANCE: Geonosian hives

HOMEWORLD: Geonosis
ABILITIES: Armed and unarmed combat, natural armor, flight

Geonosian drones make up the lowest castes of their hives, serving Geonosis' ruling queens and aristocrats as soldiers, pilots, and laborers. They are clever warriors, fighting with sonic blasters and force pikes, and are capable pilots. Clone troopers deride Geonosians as "bugs" but respect them in battle.

ZOMBIE GEONOSIAN

SPECIES: Geonosian (zombie)
HEIGHT: 1.7 m (5 ft 7 in)
ALLEGIANCE: Geonosian hives

HOMEWORLD: Geonosis
ABILITIES: Unarmed combat

Geonosian drones have little sense of individuality, valuing the survival of their hive over the preservation of any single life. This allows brain worms to animate their dead bodies, creating shambling warriors that fight for their queens. Geonosian zombies are slow-moving and fight awkwardly, relying on numbers to swarm and destroy invaders.

BRAIN WORMS

SPECIES: Brain worm
LENGTH: 1 m (3 ft 3 in)
ALLEGIANCE: None

HOMEWORLD: Geonosis
ABILITIES: Mind control, infiltration, stealth

Geonosis' hidden queens keep many secrets, including the existence of brain worms. These parasites invade living bodies, taking control of their hosts' brains and forcing them to serve the queens. After the Second Battle of Geonosis, Ahsoka Tano has to counter a brain-worm infestation aboard a Republic ship.

UMBARAN MILITIA

SPECIES: Umbaran
HEIGHT: Varies
ALLEGIANCE: Separatists
HOMEWORLD: Umbara

ABILITIES: Stealth, armed combat, infiltration, military tactics

Umbaran soldiers defend their world against the Republic during the Clone Wars. They are fierce fighters that make clever use of Umbara's advanced technology, including a gas that increases reaction time and reduces fear when inhaled. Umbarans can see in the ultraviolet spectrum, giving them an advantage when fighting amid their planet's gloom and shadows.

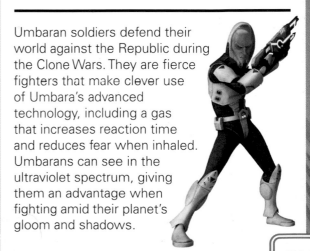

DWARF SPIDER DROID

METAL MASCOT

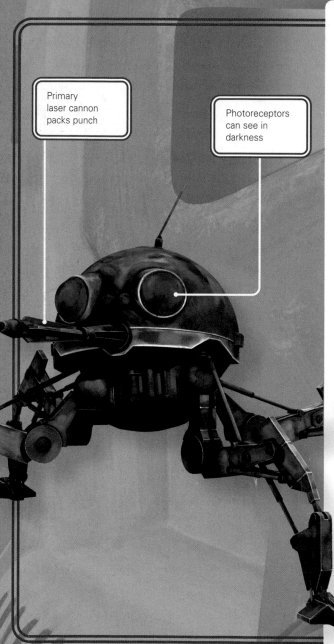

Primary laser cannon packs punch

Photoreceptors can see in darkness

MODEL: DSD1 battle droid
HEIGHT: 1.98 m (6 ft 6 in)
ALLEGIANCE: Separatists
MANUFACTURER: Baktoid Armor Workshop

ABILITIES: Heavy blaster cannon, infrared vision, climb vertical surfaces

Dwarf spider droids rely on their powerful, centrally mounted laser cannons to blast enemy troops, vehicles, and aircraft. They can see in total darkness and climb vertical surfaces, making them ideal for guard duty and reconnaissance. Dwarf spider droids are programmed to be about as smart as domesticated animals and sometimes refuse to follow dangerous orders.

"GOOD SHOT, BOY!"

– B1 battle droid

DUTIFUL DIGGERS
The DSD1 was built for the Commerce Guild and first used by the trade group to battle renegade miners deep underground. When the Guild joined the Separatist Alliance, the droid design was beefed up to deliver greater firepower. DSD1s are used to defend Teth against a raid by Jedi and clone troops.

MAGNAGUARD

BURLY BODYGUARDS

MODEL: IG-100 MagnaGuard
HEIGHT: 1.95 m (6 ft 5 in)
ALLEGIANCE: Separatists
MANUFACTURER: Holowan Mechanicals

ABILITIES: Combat abilities, magnetic feet, programmed to fight in groups, keen sensors, rugged design, piloting ability

IG-100 MagnaGuards are dangerous droids that serve top Separatist leaders as bodyguards. Even experienced Jedi hesitate to tangle with them as they are fast, programmed to fight in groups, and tough to destroy. They can keep fighting even after losing limbs or heads, and many bear scars from previous battles.

> "OK, STICK-TINNIES—YOU'RE GOING BACK TO DOOKU IN PIECES!"
> — Ahsoka Tano

TATOOINE BRAWL
MagnaGuards attack Anakin Skywalker's freighter, the *Twilight*, above Tatooine and intercept Ahsoka Tano as she tries to return Rotta the Huttlet to his father, Jabba, outside his palace. Ahsoka finds the droids faster and nimbler than she expected but manages to fight them off and reunite the Hutts.

Armor plates shield internal connectors

Electrostaff can stun or strike a deadly blow

COMMANDO DROID

MODEL: BX-series commando droid
HEIGHT: 1.91 m (6 ft 3 in)
ALLEGIANCE: Separatists
MANUFACTURER: Baktoid Combat Automata
ABILITIES: Infiltration, combat programming, agility

Commando droids are faster, more agile, and smarter than their battle-droid cousins, and clone troopers regard them with hard-earned respect. Fortunately for the Republic, Separatist officers have relatively few of these dangerous droids at their disposal and reserve them for missions that demand stealth and speed, such as the invasion of the listening post on the Rishi Moon.

COMMANDO DROID CAPTAIN

MODEL: BX-series commando droid
HEIGHT: 1.91 m (6 ft 3 in)
ALLEGIANCE: Separatists
MANUFACTURER: Baktoid Combat Automata
ABILITIES: Infiltration, combat programming, agility, leadership

Commando droid captains are distinguished from regular units by markings on their heads and chests. Some have augmented programming that gives them an advantage in tactics, improvisation, and leading other droids. Such improvements make commando-droid squads even more dangerous to clone troopers defending Republic worlds.

> Midsection accordion armor offers flexibility

CRAB DROID

MODEL: LM-432 crab droid
LENGTH: 1.49 m (4 ft 11 in)
ALLEGIANCE: Separatists
MANUFACTURER: Techno Union
ABILITIES: Combat programming, agility, vacuum pump/sprayer

Crab droids are fearsome opponents in muddy or swampy terrain, hiding in the muck and then scooting out to attack. Larger models exist but are relatively rare. Veteran clone troopers avoid crab droids' guns by jumping on top of their heads and firing down at them—but many are cut down before getting close enough to use this combat tactic.

OCTUPTARRA TRI-DROID

MODEL: Octuptarra-series combat tri-droid
HEIGHT: 3.6 m (11 ft 10 in)
ALLEGIANCE: Separatists

MANUFACTURER: Techno Union
ABILITIES: Agility, combat programming, 360-degree vision

Tri-droids are terrifying combat units that stride across battlefields on three legs, raking enemies with fire. Some models can spray virus-laden gas at Republic positions. Octuptarras are eight-eyed creatures native to Skako, which these droids resemble. The massive magna tri-droid model is 15 meters (49 feet) high and poses an even tougher threat to clone troopers in battle.

BUZZ DROID

MODEL: Pistoeka sabotage droid
HEIGHT: 0.25 m (10 in)
ALLEGIANCE: Separatists

MANUFACTURER: Colicoid Creation Nest
ABILITIES: Sabotage, magnetic grip

Buzz droids are tiny saboteurs encased in armored shells. They burst out of carrier missiles, seeking out nearby Republic ships and fighters and tearing into their hulls with drills, pincers, and saws. Anakin Skywalker tangles with buzz droids at Cato Neimoidia and later faces clouds of these vandals alongside Obi-Wan Kenobi above Coruscant. They can be knocked offline by a blow to their center eye.

D-WING AIR SECURITY DROID

MODEL: D1-series aerial battle droid
HEIGHT: 2.06 m (6 ft 9 in)
ALLEGIANCE: Separatists

MANUFACTURER: Techno Union
ABILITIES: Combat programming, security, aerial maneuvers

Experimental D-wing droids defend the Techno Union's research labs on the planet Skako Minor. Fold-out wings make them agile fliers, and their arms have built-in blaster cannons. Anakin Skywalker and the Bad Batch must fight past D-wing squads to escape after rescuing a clone from Separatist captivity. They then fight D-wings sent to attack a Poletec village.

SD-K4 ASSASSIN DROID

MODEL: SD-K4 assassin droid
HEIGHT: 1.21 m (4 ft)
ALLEGIANCE: Separatists

MANUFACTURER: Baktoid Combat Automata
ABILITIES: Infiltration, onboard mini-probes

Assassin probes are yet another fiendish design cooked up in the Techno Union's laboratories. These spiderlike droids are fast and powerful, concealing themselves and striking with legs like razors. They also carry mini-probes that creep out to overwhelm their targets if the mother unit is disabled.

MINI-ASSASSIN DROID

MODEL: SD-K4a mini-assassin droid
WIDTH: 0.14 m (6 in)
ALLEGIANCE: Separatists

MANUFACTURER: Baktoid Combat Automata
ABILITIES: Infiltration, combat, agility

SD-K4a mini-probes ride in hatches aboard their mother units, deploying and scattering according to their programming or if the main droid is disarmed. While lacking the power of full-size probes, their speed lets them swarm opponents, closing in and then slashing away with their sharp legs in a nightmarish assault.

SEPARATIST PROBE DROID

MODEL: Ringneck recon droid
HEIGHT: 1 m (3 ft 3 in)
ALLEGIANCE: Separatists

MANUFACTURER: Arakyd Industries
ABILITIES: Reconnaissance, infiltration, surveillance, combat

Probe droids are used by both sides during the Clone Wars. They are typically designed for stealth, spying on enemies, and relaying data to commanders. Separatist probe droids come in a variety of sizes. One of the most feared is the Ringneck recon droid, which helps defend Lola Sayu.

THE DECIMATOR

MODEL: Prototype S/D Decimator droid
HEIGHT: 0.35 m (1 ft 2 in)
ALLEGIANCE: Techno Union

MANUFACTURER: Baktoid Innovations
ABILITIES: Detect organic matter, destructive energy, laser cutter

The Techno Union's research scientists constantly work on new droid designs to help the Separatists. On Skako Minor, Anakin Skywalker and the Bad Batch battle with the Decimator. This prototype droid hunts organic life and then fries it with energy bursts, cutting through doors and walls in pursuit of its prey.

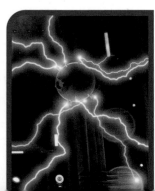

AQUA DROID

MODEL: AQ-series battle droid
HEIGHT: 2.83 m (9 ft 3 in)
ALLEGIANCE: Separatists

MANUFACTURER: Haor Chall Engineering
ABILITIES: Heavy weapons, aggressive programming, aquatic maneuvering

The Techno Union adapts the B2 Super Battle Droid to create the Aqua Droid, a model made for underwater combat. Aqua Droids are more streamlined and agile than their burly cousins but no less aggressive or dangerous, as Republic troops discover on Mon Cala and Kamino.

MILLICREEP DROID

MODEL: Scutiger-100 stealth droid
LENGTH: 0.89 m (2 ft 11 in)
ALLEGIANCE: Umbarans

MANUFACTURER: Ghost Armaments
ABILITIES: Infiltration, electroshock

Umbaran scientists are renowned for creating advanced weapons, vehicles, and droids, which they are reluctant to reveal to outsiders. During the Republic invasion of Umbara, millicreep droids slip through the clones' lines, fatally shocking several troopers before being detected and destroyed.

DEMOLITION DROID

MODEL: Custom-modified intruder droid
HEIGHT: 2.83 m (9 ft 3 in)
ALLEGIANCE: Separatists

MANUFACTURER: LIN Demolitionmech
ABILITIES: Infiltration, combat, sabotage

These intruder droids have been modified by the Separatists for a mission to strike at the heart of the Republic. They appear to be common sweeper droids but emerge from their shells to reveal their true forms. Six destroy a key power hub, leaving parts of Coruscant in darkness.

RETAIL CAUCUS DROID

MODEL: LR-57 combat/retail droid
HEIGHT: 2.58 m (8 ft 6 in)
ALLEGIANCE: Retail Caucus

MANUFACTURER: Retail Caucus
ABILITIES: Sensors, blaster cannons

The commercial guild, known as the Retail Caucus, designed the LR-57 combat droid to defend its key facilities. The droids bury themselves and wait until their antennae detect intruders, then erupt from beneath the ground to ambush their enemies. Anakin and Ahsoka run into these deadly droids during the Battle of Christophsis.

TACTICAL DROID

BRAINY BATTLE DROID

Color schemes vary between units

MODEL: T-series military strategic analysis and tactics droid
HEIGHT: 1.93 m (6 ft 4 in)
ALLEGIANCE: Separatists

MANUFACTURER: Baktoid Combat Automata
ABILITIES: Armor, leadership, strategic programming

Tactical droids are smart mechanicals programmed to analyze battles, calculate odds, and adjust strategies in real time. They are often found aboard Droid Control Ships or surveying battlefields from mobile headquarters. From there, they give orders to B1 battle droids, which perform poorly when faced with situations not covered by their programming.

CRUNCHING THE NUMBERS

Tactical droids are extremely arrogant machines. They are confident in their calculations and are convinced that organic beings are too flawed to be trusted with the science of war. They often argue with Separatist commanders, insisting that their tactics are flawless and must be used in battle.

"I AM A DROID. I AM ALWAYS RIGHT."
– Tactical Droid TX-20

SUPER TACTICAL DROID

CEREBRAL COMMANDER

MODEL: ST-series military strategic analysis and tactics droid
HEIGHT: 1.94 m (6 ft 4 in)
ALLEGIANCE: Separatists

MANUFACTURER: Baktoid Combat Automata
ABILITIES: Armor, leadership, enhanced strategic programming, resistance to interrogation

Super tactical droids are enhanced versions of tactical droids that improve on their predecessors' shortcomings. They are better at analyzing tactics and predicting how organic commanders will respond to events. Super tactical droids develop personalities, and some units, such as Onderon's General Kalani, give themselves names instead of numbers.

"IT IS ONLY A MATTER OF TIME BEFORE THEY ARE ELIMINATED."
– General Kalani

RUTHLESS LEADERS
Super tactical droids are programmed to serve as generals and admirals in the Separatist war machine. They are ruthless and calculating but arrogant and overconfident like earlier tactical models.

Status indicator for central processing hub

These droid units often choose personalized color schemes

CAD BANE

HUNTER FOR HIRE

Bane fights with custom Persuader blasters

SPECIES: Duros
HEIGHT: 1.85 m (6 ft 1 in)
ALLEGIANCE: None
HOMEWORLD: Duro

ABILITIES: Armed and unarmed combat, aerial combat, infiltration, tactics, starfighter piloting

Cad Bane is a merciless Duros bounty hunter, famed for his willingness to hunt down any fugitive or break into any stronghold, no matter how dangerous the job. All that matters to Bane is that the price is right, and given his reputation in the galactic underworld, he is able to charge top credit. Clients sometimes grumble at the cost, but if they want the best, they come to Bane.

"AS LONG AS I GET PAID, IT MAKES NO DIFFERENCE TO ME."

– Cad Bane

READY FOR ANYTHING

Bane's standard gear is tailored to a range of situations. Breathing tubes maintain his oxygen supply in non-oxygen atmospheres, and rocket boots help him match a Jedi's agility and speed. Bane respects the Jedi but thinks they're too quick to rely on the Force, which can make them careless in battle.

BOBA FETT

A LONELY LEGACY

SPECIES: Human (unaltered clone)
HEIGHT: 1.35 m (4 ft 5 in)
ALLEGIANCE: None

HOMEWORLD: Kamino
ABILITIES: Assassination, combat, leadership, military tactics, starship piloting

Helmet offers atmosphere filter and enhanced vision

Boba is an unaltered clone of Jango Fett, who raised him on Kamino and introduced him to the bounty-hunting trade. Boba witnessed Jango's death on Geonosis at the hands of Mace Windu and vowed to take revenge. After that quest fails, he follows in his father's footsteps, putting together a crew and becoming a star bounty hunter despite his youth.

LEARNING THE ROPES
After Jango's death, Boba learns the art of bounty hunting from Aurra Sing, who also teaches him tough lessons in being ruthless. Older and harder, Boba then assembles his own Tatooine-based crew, leading a posse that includes Bossk, Dengar, C-21 Highsinger, Latts Razzi, and Asajj Ventress.

"YOU DOUBLE-CROSS ME AGAIN, YOU'LL PAY FOR IT."

– Boba Fett

BOSSK

TRANDOSHAN WITH A TEMPER

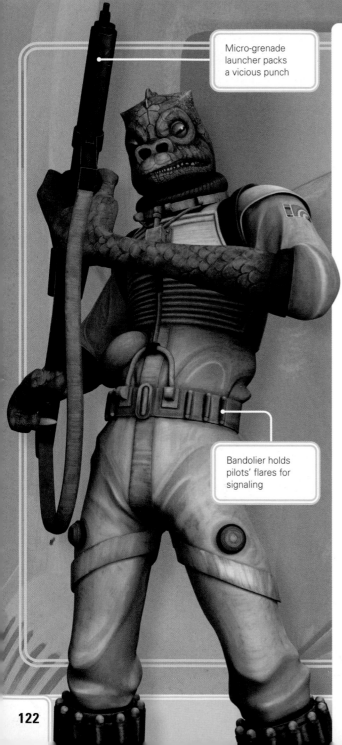

Micro-grenade launcher packs a vicious punch

Bandolier holds pilots' flares for signaling

SPECIES: Trandoshan
HEIGHT: 1.9 m (6 ft 3 in)
ALLEGIANCE: None
HOMEWORLD: Trandosha

ABILITIES: Armed combat, tracking, infiltration, starship piloting, regeneration

Reptilian bounty hunter Bossk helps Boba Fett track down and target Jedi Master Mace Windu. The mission fails, but Bossk sees something in the young hunter, becoming his bodyguard in a Republic prison and a member of his crew. A gifted tracker, Bossk draws on his natural Trandoshan instincts to locate fugitives.

> **"YOU GOT A PROBLEM WITH BOBA, YOU GOT A PROBLEM WITH ME."**
>
> – Bossk

A HARDY HUNTER

Like all Trandoshans, Bossk can regenerate damage to his scaly body—even regrowing missing limbs. But regeneration is slow and painful, and a missing limb suggests that a Trandoshan hunter was defeated by their prey. Bossk would rather keep all of his arms and legs firmly attached.

AURRA SING

DEADLY HUNTER

SPECIES: Palliduvan
HEIGHT: 1.83 m (6 ft)
ALLEGIANCE: None
HOMEWORLD: Nar Shaddaa

ABILITIES: Expert sniper, armed and unarmed combat, assassination, infiltration, surveillance, starship piloting

Antenna connects to biocomputer

Well-worn boots made from rancor hide

Master assassin and sniper Aurra Sing is one of the galaxy's most merciless bounty hunters, and her name alone sows dread among her peers. She counts abductions, raids, and assassination attempts on politicians like Padmé Amidala as merely a fast route to a big paycheck. Aurra's list of underworld associates includes Hondo Ohnaka, Cad Bane, and Boba Fett.

AN EXPERT SNIPER
Aurra can hit targets from incredible distances using her Czerka Adventurer rifle. An antenna in her head connects to a built-in biocomputer that she uses to eavesdrop on conversations and monitor communications—giving her an early warning that authorities are closing in on her position.

"MY EMPLOYER WANTS TO GET EVEN WITH YOU. SIMPLE AS THAT."

– Aurra Sing

EMBO

SPECIES: Kyuzo
HEIGHT: 1.99 m (6 ft 6 in)
ALLEGIANCE: None
HOMEWORLD: Phatrong

ABILITIES: Armed and unarmed combat, infiltration, tracking, sharpshooting, agility

Kyuzo war helmet is both weapon and shield

Embo is a hulking Kyuzo bounty hunter with a fearsome reputation as an expert tracker, sniper, and muscle for hire. He is known for his distinctive war helmet, which doubles as a boomerang-style weapon and a shield, and for his deadly pet, an anooba named Marrok.

Embo has no code beyond getting paid. He works alongside Anakin Skywalker as part of Sugi's crew on Felucia but later battles the Jedi in pursuit of Rush Clovis on Scipio. Near the end of the Clone Wars, he joins up with the mercenary crew led by young Boba Fett.

Convinced this time his luck will change

GREEDO

SPECIES: Rodian
HEIGHT: 1.74 m (5 ft 9 in)
ALLEGIANCE: None
HOMEWORLD: Tatooine

ABILITIES: Armed and unarmed combat, infrared vision, sense vibrations

Greedo dreams of making a name for himself as a bounty hunter despite seemingly endless bad luck and a reputation for being careless and irresponsible. Ignoring evidence that he should pursue a different line of work, he remains on Tatooine hoping for his big break.

Greedo usually works for Jabba the Hutt but agrees to kidnap Baron Papanoida's daughters for the Trade Federation. As usual, things go wrong for Greedo: Papanoida traces him to Tatooine; an angry Jabba insists he produce the missing girls, and he barely survives a cantina shootout.

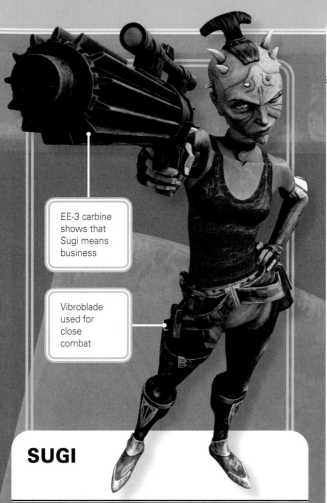

EE-3 carbine shows that Sugi means business

Vibroblade used for close combat

DENGAR

SPECIES: Human
HEIGHT: 1.87 m (6 ft 2 in)
ALLEGIANCE: None
HOMEWORLD: Corellia

ABILITIES: Armed and unarmed combat, infiltration

Dengar was a gladiator on Corellia before becoming a bounty hunter and is known for his white-and-brown turban and his pitted battle armor. He rushes into battle with a joy that makes veteran mercenaries wonder about his life expectancy.

Dengar is part of Boba Fett's crew when the young hunter agrees to protect a subtram on Quarzite. He's assigned to guard the rear of the tram with Asajj Ventress, who proves immune to his attempts at charm in the brief period before Kage warriors attack.

DLT-18 blaster rifle packs heavy firepower

Plated battle armor for protection in combat

SUGI

SPECIES: Zabrak
HEIGHT: 1.82 m (6 ft)
ALLEGIANCE: None
HOMEWORLD: Iridonia

ABILITIES: Armed and unarmed combat, infiltration, tracking, starship piloting, leadership

Sugi is a Zabrak bounty hunter who signs on with her crew—Embo, Seripas, and Rumi Paramita—to protect a Felucian farm village from Hondo Ohnaka's pirates. She's a rare example of an honorable mercenary: when Hondo tries to bribe her into moving on, Sugi refuses, keeping her word to the villagers.

Sugi's crew decides to join forces with Anakin Skywalker's party of Jedi and drives Hondo's gang away. Later, she is hired by Kashyyyk's Chieftain Tarfful to rescue Chewbacca from the moon Wasskah and provides security for the Grand Hutt Council.

LATTS RAZZI

SPECIES: Theelin
HEIGHT: 1.79 m (5 ft 10 in)
ALLEGIANCE: None
HOMEWORLD: Korbori

ABILITIES: Armed and unarmed combat, martial arts, tracking, infiltration

Latts Razzi is a deadly Theelin mercenary whose services command top credit. She wears a boa made of scales which can be formed into a whip or lasso. Latts joins Boba Fett's crew to protect a subtram on Quarzite and then to raid Count Dooku's fortress on Serenno in an attempt to free the maverick Jedi Quinlan Vos.

RUMI PARAMITA

Form-fitting gear allows freedom of movement

SPECIES: Frenk
HEIGHT: 2.15 m (7 ft 1 in)
ALLEGIANCE: None
HOMEWORLD: Gorobei

ABILITIES: Armed and unarmed combat, sharpshooting, infiltration, tracking

Rumi Paramita is an expert sniper who signs on with Sugi to protect farmers in the village of Akira on Felucia. She fires at Hondo Ohnaka's pirates as they attack, but Rumi is killed by a blast from Hondo's tank—a fatal shot fired by a Kowakian monkey-lizard, of all things. It's a sad end for a skilled hunter.

C-21 HIGHSINGER

MODEL: Heavily modified combat droid
HEIGHT: 2.25 m (7 ft 5 in)
ALLEGIANCE: None

MANUFACTURER: Unknown
ABILITIES: Armed and unarmed combat, martial arts, agility, tracking

C-21 Highsinger is a highly modified droid of uncertain origin. What no one doubts is that Highsinger is a terrifyingly efficient combat machine with superhuman reflexes and speed. He values his independence but agrees to work with Boba Fett's crew on several occasions, providing firepower for missions on Quarzite and Serenno.

CATO PARASITTI

Ammo kept in utility pouch

SPECIES: Clawdite
HEIGHT: 1.79 m (5 ft 10 in)
ALLEGIANCE: None
HOMEWORLD: Zolan

ABILITIES: Shape-shifting, infiltration, surveillance, armed and unarmed combat, agility, data slicing

Cad Bane hires Cato Parasitti to infiltrate the Jedi Temple on Coruscant as part of his plan to steal a Holocron from the Order's vaults. The Clawdite shape-shifter assumes the form of the murdered Jedi Master Ord Enisence and then archivist Jocasta Nu. Ahsoka Tano discovers the ruse and Parasitti is captured, but Bane manages to get away with his prize.

CASTAS

SPECIES: Klatooinian
HEIGHT: 1.99 m (6 ft 6 in)
ALLEGIANCE: None
HOMEWORLD: Klatooine

ABILITIES: Armed and unarmed combat, intimidation

Castas is a beefy Klatooinian mercenary who is hired with Aurra Sing and Bossk to help Boba Fett take revenge against Mace Windu. But Castas soon tires of obeying orders and decides taking on the Republic Navy is far too risky. He decides to go his own way when the crew reaches Florrum, but Sing catches him in the act of selling her out and guns him down.

SERIPAS

Coverall also available in small size

SPECIES: Ssori
HEIGHT: 0.74 m (2 ft 5 in)
ALLEGIANCE: None
HOMEWORLD: Ssori Fragments

ABILITIES: Armed and unarmed combat, powered exoskeleton

Bounty hunter Seripas appears as a massive figure in heavy armor, striding across Felucia's nysillim fields as part of Sugi's crew. But Ahsoka Tano soon discovers this mercenary isn't what she perceives: the imposing armor is really a powered exoskeleton driven by a smaller being. When Seripas' armor proves too bulky, he sheds it and fights as his true self.

TODO 360

MODEL: Unknown
HEIGHT: 0.66 m (2 ft 2 in)
ALLEGIANCE: None
MANUFACTURER: Vertseth Automata
ABILITIES: Infiltration, maintenance

Todo 360 assists Cad Bane and Cato Parasitti in stealing a Holocron from the Jedi Temple, posing as a maintenance droid and disabling the security systems. He is torn apart by a bomb Bane put inside him as a fail-safe but rebuilt in time to help Bane free Ziro the Hutt from Republic captivity.

KRONOS-327

MODEL: IG-86 sentinel droid
HEIGHT: 1.96 m (6 ft 5 in)
ALLEGIANCE: None
MANUFACTURER: Holowan Laboratories
ABILITIES: Combat, military tactics, security, piloting, data slicing

KRONOS-327 is one of Ziro the Hutt's most trusted assassin droids, but his long record of success means nothing when he fails to complete a mission in the Yout system. Angered by KRONOS' failure, Ziro orders that the droid be reduced to spare parts.

HELIOS-3D

MODEL: IG-86 sentinel droid
HEIGHT: 1.96 m (6 ft 5 in)
ALLEGIANCE: None
MANUFACTURER: Holowan Laboratories
ABILITIES: Combat, military tactics, security, piloting, data slicing

HELIOS-3D is a sentinel droid who assists Cad Bane in his raid on the Senate. He drives the speeder that ferries Ziro the Hutt away from a Republic prison, ignoring the Hutt's demands that his droid driver take him to the Outer Rim at once.

HELIOS-3E

MODEL: IG-86 sentinel droid
HEIGHT: 1.96 m (6 ft 5 in)
ALLEGIANCE: None
MANUFACTURER: Holowan Laboratories
ABILITIES: Combat, military tactics, security, piloting, data slicing

HELIOS-3E serves Cad Bane as he prepares to free Ziro the Hutt from a prison on Coruscant. HELIOS brings C-3PO to Bane for interrogation and then tracks down R2-D2. Once Bane extracts the information he needs from the droids, HELIOS dumps them on the street.

ROBONINO

SPECIES: Patrolian
HEIGHT: 1.27 m (4 ft 2 in)
ALLEGIANCE: None
HOMEWORLD: Patrolia

ABILITIES: Infiltration, data slicing, sabotage, explosives handling

Robonino is a skilled slicer and saboteur who infiltrates the Senate Building on Coruscant as part of Cad Bane's raid. Robonino manages to ambush and capture Anakin Skywalker, shocking the Jedi until he loses consciousness.

DERROWN

SPECIES: Parwan
HEIGHT: 2.21 m (7 ft 3 in)
ALLEGIANCE: None
HOMEWORLD: Parwa

ABILITIES: Armed and unarmed combat, electric shock, aerial maneuvers, infiltration

Derrown's gas-filled body can float, and his tendrils deliver deadly shocks, earning him the grim nickname of the Exterminator. He passes Count Dooku's tests in a bounty hunter's testing ground named the Box. Derrown joins the strike team targeting Chancellor Palpatine on Naboo but is neutralized by Obi-Wan Kenobi.

RAKO HARDEEN

SPECIES: Human
HEIGHT: 1.89 m (6 ft 2 in)
ALLEGIANCE: None
HOMEWORLD: Concord Dawn

ABILITIES: Armed and unarmed combat, sharpshooting, infiltration, tracking

Rako Hardeen is a bounty hunter known for his skill as a sniper. He is apprehended by the Jedi on Coruscant and held captive while Obi-Wan Kenobi assumes his identity in order to gain a place on a strike team seeking to kidnap Chancellor Palpatine during a visit to Naboo.

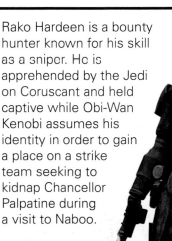

SHAHAN ALAMA

SPECIES: Weequay
HEIGHT: 1.85 m (6 ft 1 in)
ALLEGIANCE: None
HOMEWORLD: Sriluur

ABILITIES: Armed and unarmed combat, infiltration, tracking

Shahan Alama is a former pirate who joins Cad Bane's raid on the Senate Building. She is observant, noting that a droid destroyed by Anakin Skywalker shows no lightsaber damage and correctly concluding the Jedi isn't carrying his laser sword.

JAKOLI

SPECIES: Rodian
HEIGHT: 1.74 m (5 ft 9 in)
ALLEGIANCE: None
HOMEWORLD: Rodia

ABILITIES: Armed and unarmed combat, infrared vision, sense vibrations, sharpshooter, tracking, infiltration

Jakoli is a Rodian bounty hunter known for his refusal to take bounties alive, a policy that gives him a fearsome reputation. He answers Count Dooku's call to be tested in the Box but dies when he is fatally shocked in a close encounter with a ray shield.

MANTU

SPECIES: Selkath
HEIGHT: 1.54 m (5 ft 1 in)
ALLEGIANCE: None
HOMEWORLD: Manaan

ABILITIES: Armed and unarmed combat, infiltration, tracking

The Selkath are a peaceful people, but the bounty hunter Mantu is an exception who is known as a heartless killer. Mantu falls victim to ray shields in trying to prove himself in Count Dooku's fiendish Box. He falls to his death after a shield delivers an incapacitating shock.

SINRICH

SPECIES: Snivvian
HEIGHT: 1.74 m (5 ft 9 in)
ALLEGIANCE: None
HOMEWORLD: Cadomai Prime

ABILITIES: Armed and unarmed combat, engineering, mechanical repairs, data slicing, infiltration, sabotage

Sinrich is a skilled technician and famed as the inventor of the holographic disguise matrix—a useful tool for bounty hunters and infiltrators. He dies trying to escape the Box, but Count Dooku's team uses Sinrich's invention when targeting Chancellor Palpatine during his visit to Naboo.

TWAZZI

SPECIES: Frenk
HEIGHT: 2.11 m (6 ft 11 in)
ALLEGIANCE: None
HOMEWORLD: Gorobei

ABILITIES: Armed and unarmed combat, agility, infiltration

Twazzi is an acrobatic bounty hunter who beats Count Dooku's tests in the Box and joins the mission to abduct Chancellor Palpatine on Naboo. She uses Sinrich's holographic disguise matrix to pose as Palpatine, but Anakin Skywalker discovers the trick. Twazzi loses her right arm and is arrested.

KIERA SWAN

SPECIES: Weequay
HEIGHT: 1.68 m (5 ft 6 in)
ALLEGIANCE: None
HOMEWORLD: Sriluur

ABILITIES: Armed and unarmed combat, starship piloting, agility, infiltration

Kiera Swan is a former pirate who makes her living as a bounty hunter despite having a price on her own head. She is a skilled hunter with two victories in the hunters' competition known as the Obsidian Sphere. The Box proves beyond her skills, as Kiera dies trying to evade its laser-blade gauntlet.

SIXTAT

SPECIES: Sakiyan
HEIGHT: 1.84 m (6 ft)
ALLEGIANCE: None
HOMEWORLD: Saki

ABILITIES: Armed and unarmed combat, infiltration, keen senses, tracking, sharpshooting

Sixtat is a talented sniper known as the Outlands Butcher, an ugly nickname he wears with pride. He swaggers into the Box certain that he will pass its deadly tests but falters in the final challenge. Sixtat makes his first two shots but misses the third and is dropped into a fiery pit, ending his life.

ONCA

SPECIES: Ithorian
HEIGHT: 2.05 m (6 ft 9 in)
ALLEGIANCE: None
HOMEWORLD: Ithor

ABILITIES: Armed combat, tracking

Onca and his brother Bulduga earn their living as bounty hunters. They have a reputation for teamwork but prove unequal to the perils of the Box. Bulduga dies before the tests begin, while Onca quickly succumbs to a laser blade, ending the brothers' careers.

BULDUGA

SPECIES: Ithorian
HEIGHT: 2.27 m (7 ft 5 in)
ALLEGIANCE: None
HOMEWORLD: Ithor

ABILITIES: Armed combat, tracking

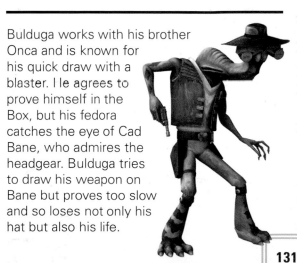

Bulduga works with his brother Onca and is known for his quick draw with a blaster. He agrees to prove himself in the Box, but his fedora catches the eye of Cad Bane, who admires the headgear. Bulduga tries to draw his weapon on Bane but proves too slow and so loses not only his hat but also his life.

HONDO OHNAKA

SCOURGE OF THE SPACEWAYS

Pigtails are high fashion for pirates

SPECIES: Weequay
HEIGHT: 1.85 m (6 ft 1 in)
ALLEGIANCE: Neutral
HOMEWORLD: Sriluur

ABILITIES: Combat, leadership, striking business deals, persuasion, thinking and talking fast

Hondo Ohnaka makes a dishonest living smuggling, stealing, and kidnapping across the Outer Rim. A charming rogue, he's always friendly and cheerful, delighted to see old friends and foes again—and just as happy to rob them blind if given the chance. As Hondo sees it, it's a tough Galaxy, so you should live for today and not worry too much about tomorrow.

> "YOU KNOW WHAT I ALWAYS SAY: SPEAK SOFTLY AND DRIVE A BIG TANK."
>
> – Hondo Ohnaka

FRIENDS, ENEMIES, AND IN BETWEEN

Hondo crosses paths with Obi-Wan Kenobi, Anakin Skywalker, and Ahsoka Tano as both friends and foes. He also attracts the wrath of Maul, Count Dooku, and General Grievous. Such perilous situations threaten not just his profits but also his life, the only thing Hondo values more than a big payday.

JABBA THE HUTT

GALACTIC GANGSTER

SPECIES: Hutt
HEIGHT: 1.95 m (6 ft 5 in)
ALLEGIANCE: Hutt clans
HOMEWORLD: Nal Hutta

ABILITIES: Leadership, intimidation, business acumen, political influence

Jabba the Hutt rules over his criminal empire from a desert fortress on Tatooine. He controls strategic Outer Rim trade routes and builds a web of unsavory businesses, from spice to slaves. Jabba sees other beings as nothing more than sources of profit. He respects strength and daring over goodness and honesty, making and breaking deals for his own benefit.

PULLED INTO WAR
Jabba is drawn into the Clone Wars when the Separatists kidnap his infant son, Rotta, and frame the Republic for the crime. Later, Maul's troops storm Jabba's palace and force him to become part of the Shadow Collective. Jabba agrees and bides his time—certain Maul will go too far and fall as quickly as he rose.

"OH HO HO HO."

— Jabba the Hutt

Sneer of displeasure

Thick, muscular body contains no skeleton

ZIRO THE HUTT

SPECIES: Hutt
HEIGHT: 3.9 m (12 ft 10 in)
ALLEGIANCE: None
HOMEWORLD: Coruscant

ABILITIES: Persuasion, intimidation, leadership

Ziro the Hutt is Jabba's uncle and the leader of a criminal syndicate on Coruscant. He conspires with Count Dooku to kidnap Jabba's son Rotta, a plot that lands Ziro in a Republic prison. The Hutt Council hires Cad Bane to free Ziro and jails him on Nal Hutta. He escapes but is killed by an old flame, Sy Snootles, on Jabba's orders.

GORGA THE HUTT

SPECIES: Hutt
HEIGHT: 3.6 m (11 ft 10 in)
ALLEGIANCE: Hutt clans
HOMEWORLD: Nal Hutta

ABILITIES: Persuasion, negotiations, accounting

Gorga the Hutt is Jabba's nephew and serves as the Hutt Council's accountant. He ensures the clans' criminal enterprises keep their coffers full of credits. Gorga wears a monocle and headset that can access Hutt datafeeds, allowing him to keep track of important business during the clans' lengthy meetings and parties.

ROTTA THE HUTTLET

SPECIES: Hutt
HEIGHT: 0.43 m (1 ft 5 in)
ALLEGIANCE: Hutt clans
HOMEWORLD: Tatooine

ABILITIES: Family connections

Rotta the Huttlet is Jabba's baby son and a pawn in the Clone Wars. When Asajj Ventress Huttnaps him from Tatooine on Count Dooku's orders, Dooku blames the crime on the Republic. Anakin Skywalker and Ahsoka Tano rescue Rotta on Teth and risk their lives to return him to Jabba.

GARDULLA THE HUTT

SPECIES: Hutt
HEIGHT: 3.7 m (12 ft 2 in)
ALLEGIANCE: Hutt clans
HOMEWORLD: Nal Hutta

ABILITIES: Persuasion, intimidation, leadership

Gardulla the Hutt is a crime lord who sits on the Hutt Council. She has palaces on Nal Hutta and Tatooine and enslaved Shmi and Anakin Skywalker until she lost them to junk dealer Watto in a wager. Ziro the Hutt is imprisoned in Gardulla's Nal Hutta palace until Sy Snootles breaks him out of jail.

MAMA THE HUTT

SPECIES: Hutt
HEIGHT: 3.61 m (11 ft 10 in)
ALLEGIANCE: None
HOMEWORLD: Nal Hutta

ABILITIES: Persuasion, intimidation

Mama the Hutt is a clan matriarch related to many Hutt crime lords. She dwells in her house in Nal Hutta's swamps, carefully tending to the needs of her menagerie of Sha'rellian toops and shooing away nosy bounty hunters, arrogant Jedi, and needy relatives.

AROK THE HUTT

SPECIES: Hutt
HEIGHT: 2.09 m (6 ft 10 in)
ALLEGIANCE: Hutt clans
HOMEWORLD: A-Foroon

ABILITIES: Persuasion, intimidation, leadership

Arok the Hutt leads one of the Five Hutt Families and sits on the Hutt Council. His many bad habits include enjoying smelly Sakiyan cheroots, to the annoyance of his fellow Hutts. After Maul and Death Watch storm the council chambers, Arok reluctantly agrees to join Maul's new Shadow Collective.

MARLO THE HUTT

SPECIES: Hutt
HEIGHT: 2.29 m (7 ft 6 in)
ALLEGIANCE: Hutt clans
HOMEWORLD: Nal Hutta

ABILITIES: Persuasion, intimidation, leadership

Marlo the Hutt is a member of the Hutt Council and a high-ranking clan leader in the Five Hutt Families. He wears a Sha'rellian toop atop his head, pampering the creature to ensure his grooming is impeccable. He agrees to join Maul's Shadow Collective after the former Sith makes an offer the Hutts can't refuse.

ORUBA THE HUTT

SPECIES: Hutt
HEIGHT: 2.02 m (6 ft 8 in)
ALLEGIANCE: Hutt clans
HOMEWORLD: Nal Hutta

ABILITIES: Persuasion, intimidation, leadership

Oruba the Hutt is one of the Council's most respected Hutts, held in high esteem for his wisdom and ruthlessness. He wears a jaunty hat and wrap to protect his skin, which is pigment-free due to a genetic mutation. Savage Opress executes Oruba when Maul and Death Watch invade the Hutt council chamber.

PILF MUKMUK

Carefully groomed neck ruff

SPECIES: Kowakian monkey-lizard
HEIGHT: 0.58 m (1 ft 11 in)
ALLEGIANCE: Hondo Ohnaka's gang

HOMEWORLD: Florrum
ABILITIES: Infiltration, theft, mimicry

Pilf Mukmuk is Hondo Ohnaka's prized pet, a cackling mascot who can be found wandering around Florrum's pirate base getting into trouble. After Count Dooku is captured on Vanqor, Pilf rummages through his pockets, taking the Sith Lord's priceless lightsaber. Pilf has a yellow-pigmented brother known as Pikk, who is an expert spy and sneak.

GWARM

SPECIES: Weequay
HEIGHT: 1.92 m (6 ft 4 in)
ALLEGIANCE: Hondo Ohnaka's gang

HOMEWORLD: Florrum
ABILITIES: Combat, sharpshooting, intimidation

Gwarm is one of Hondo Ohnaka's lieutenants, a swaggering pirate with no principles beyond the idea that might makes right. He lucks into a big score on Felucia, alerting Hondo that the planet's farmers grow valuable nysillim. That scheme ends badly for the pirates, but Gwarm is by Hondo's side when his gang invades a Jedi training ship in the hopes of stealing its cargo of kyber crystals.

R5-P8

MODEL: R-series astromech droid
HEIGHT: 1.25 m (4 ft 1 in)
ALLEGIANCE: Hondo Ohnaka's gang

MANUFACTURER: Industrial Automaton
ABILITIES: Starship maintenance, information retrieval, repairs, starfighter piloting, security

R5-P8 acts as a guard for Hondo Ohnaka's pirate gang, thanks to a blaster that's been wired into his logic module. This isn't exactly what he was programmed to do, but poor R-5 does his best to obey orders. Any droids the gang considers expendable often wind up being used for target practice, a fate the poor astromech would like to avoid.

Sawtooth smile drawn by bored pirate

PEG LEG PIIT

SPECIES: Weequay
HEIGHT: 1.69 m (5 ft 7 in)
ALLEGIANCE: Hondo Ohnaka's gang
HOMEWORLD: Florrum
ABILITIES: Combat, infiltration, mayhem

Peg Leg Piit is a veteran in Hondo Ohnaka's pirate gang, quick to reach for a blaster when things go wrong and a mug of grog when they go right. She helps capture Count Dooku and the two Jedi sent to retrieve him. Piit survives General Grievous' invasion of Florrum as well as Maul's raid.

Artificial leg made from phrik alloy

TURK FALSO

SPECIES: Weequay
HEIGHT: 1.92 m (6 ft 4 in)
ALLEGIANCE: Himself
HOMEWORLD: Florrum
ABILITIES: Combat, swoop piloting, scheming

Turk Falso is one of Hondo Ohnaka's lieutenants but dislikes taking the pirate chief's orders and daydreams about being his own boss. When the Republic sends a shipment of spice as ransom for Count Dooku, Turk decides to steal it and strike out on his own. His plan falls apart when Jar Jar Binks and a squad of clone troopers attack the base. Dooku then escapes, killing Falso.

PARSEL

SPECIES: Weequay
HEIGHT: 1.89 m (6 ft 2 in)
ALLEGIANCE: Hondo Ohnaka's gang
HOMEWORLD: Florrum
ABILITIES: Starship piloting, combat, intimidation

Parsel is a hulking Weequay who serves Hondo Ohnaka as both a brawler and a starship pilot. He betrays Hondo to join Maul and Savage Opress, hoping to improve his fortunes with a more powerful gang. Parsel soon realizes he's made a mistake and switches sides again, helping drive the Zabrak brothers away. Hondo forgives him: what does one expect from pirates, anyway?

ZITON MOJ

BLACK SUN LEADER

Falleen exude pheromones that can influence others

SPECIES: Falleen
HEIGHT: 1.95 m (6 ft 5 in)
ALLEGIANCE: Black Sun, Shadow Collective

HOMEWORLD: Falleen
ABILITIES: Armed and unarmed combat, martial arts, leadership, negotiation, intimidation

Ziton Moj is a brawny enforcer for the Black Sun crime syndicate. He serves the group's leaders as Captain of the Guard on Mustafar. While he enjoys cracking skulls in a good fight, he's also wise enough to know which battles he can't win. When Maul and Savage Opress do away with Black Sun's leaders, Moj swiftly switches sides, joining Maul's new Shadow Collective as a key lieutenant.

"AFTER CAREFUL CONSIDERATION, WE WILL JOIN YOU."

– Ziton Moj

LOFTY AMBITIONS
Moj serves Maul well as Black Sun's new leader, fighting alongside him as the Shadow Collective takes over Mandalore. After Maul's defeat at the hands of Darth Sidious, Moj returns to Mustafar and seeks to increase Black Sun's influence by forcing the Pykes to join him in creating a new criminal empire.

LOM PYKE

SPICE KINGPIN

SPECIES: Pyke
HEIGHT: 1.91 m (6 ft 3 in)
ALLEGIANCE: Pyke Syndicate, Shadow Collective

HOMEWORLD: Oba Diah
ABILITIES: Leadership, negotiation

Lom Pyke leads the Pyke Syndicate, a criminal gang that controls the galaxy's illegal and dangerous trade in spice. Lom rules his empire from a shadowy den on Oba Diah, where he meets with smugglers, crooked officials, and other crime bosses. He freely joins Maul's Shadow Collective in the hope of gaining power and profits.

Features are stained with spice residue

CC-420 pistol manufactured for Pykes

OLD SECRETS
Years ago at Darth Tyranus' request, the Pykes killed Jedi Sifo-Dyas, but they imprisoned the Jedi's companion, Silman, in case they need to blackmail the Sith. Near the end of the Clone Wars, the Jedi investigate Sifo-Dyas' demise, and Lom confesses the Pykes' role, seeking a pardon. Tyranus kills the traitor.

"YOU HAVE NO BUSINESS LEFT WITH THE PYKES, TYRANUS."

— Lom Pyke

DRYDEN VOS

SPECIES: Unknown
HEIGHT: 1.92 m (6 ft 4 in)
ALLEGIANCE: Crimson Dawn
HOMEWORLD: Unknown

ABILITIES: Armed and unarmed combat, leadership, negotiation, persuasion, intimidation

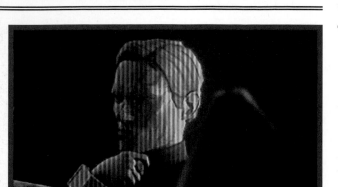

Dryden Vos is a rising star in the galactic underworld, a key leader of the crime syndicate known as Crimson Dawn, and a lieutenant in Maul's Shadow Collective. Vos is simultaneously a cold-blooded killer and a wealthy art collector, acting as a kind host one minute and then flying into a rage the next. In the final days of the Clone Wars, Maul orders Vos to go into hiding, fearing what might be coming.

XOMIT GRUNSEIT

SPECIES: Falleen
HEIGHT: 2.1 m (6 ft 11 in)
ALLEGIANCE: Black Sun
HOMEWORLD: Mustafar

ABILITIES: Armed and unarmed combat, intimidation, negotiations, persuasion, leadership

Xomit Grunseit leads the Black Sun crime syndicate and is based on Mustafar during the Clone Wars. When Maul and Savage Opress ask Grunseit to join Maul's new criminal group, named the Shadow Collective, he scoffs that Black Sun are not mercenaries and orders the visitors to be killed. His own death comes moments later: he is cut down by Savage's hurled lightsaber.

"QUIET! WE ARE THE BLACK SUN!"

– Xomit Grunseit

FIFE

SPECIES: Pyke
HEIGHT: 1.91 m (6 ft 3 in)
ALLEGIANCE: Pyke Syndicate
HOMEWORLD: Oba Diah

ABILITIES: Combat, bureaucracy, security, organization, military tactics

Fife is Marg Krim's majordomo, working to keep the Pyke Syndicate's spice smuggling on track so the crime syndicate's profits keep growing. He is also a capable warrior, fighting with the forces of the Shadow Collective on Ord Mantell and working to outmaneuver Ahsoka Tano and the Martez sisters when they try to flee Oba Diah.

MARG KRIM

SPECIES: Pyke
HEIGHT: 1.91 m (6 ft 3 in)
ALLEGIANCE: Pyke Syndicate
HOMEWORLD: Oba Diah

ABILITIES: Negotiations, persuasion, intimidation, leadership

Marg Krim becomes the leader of the Pyke Syndicate after Lom Pyke is killed by Count Dooku. Krim seeks to expand the illegal spice trade, striking deals with Kessel's elite to smuggle the valuable substance offworld. Krim takes orders from Maul, obeying his warning to keep a low profile at the end of the Clone Wars.

"DID YOU HONESTLY THINK YOU'D GET AWAY WITH FOOLING A PYKE?"

– Marg Krim

RUSH CLOVIS

SLIPPERY SENATOR

Tattoos are a sign of high status on Scipio

SPECIES: Human
HEIGHT: 1.92 m (6 ft 4 in)
ALLEGIANCE: Separatists
HOMEWORLD: Scipio

ABILITIES: Legislative knowledge, political skills, leadership, charm

Rush Clovis represents Scipio in the Senate while playing a key role in the InterGalactic Banking Clan, which lends credits to both the Republic and Separatists. He conspires with the Separatists early in the war, then becomes the Banking Clan's leader and tries to restore its independence. But others seek to control the group, and their schemes endanger both its future and Clovis' life.

> **"YOU DON'T UNDERSTAND! YOU'VE ALL BEEN DECEIVED!"**
> – Rush Clovis

A PAWN OF DOOKU

Clovis' Separatist ties ruin his reputation, but he makes an unlikely comeback, rising to head of the Banking Clan. He genuinely hopes to restore the group's neutrality but becomes a pawn in a plot to give Palpatine control of the banks. Clovis dies in the battle for Scipio.

MIRAJ SCINTEL

ZYGERRIAN QUEEN

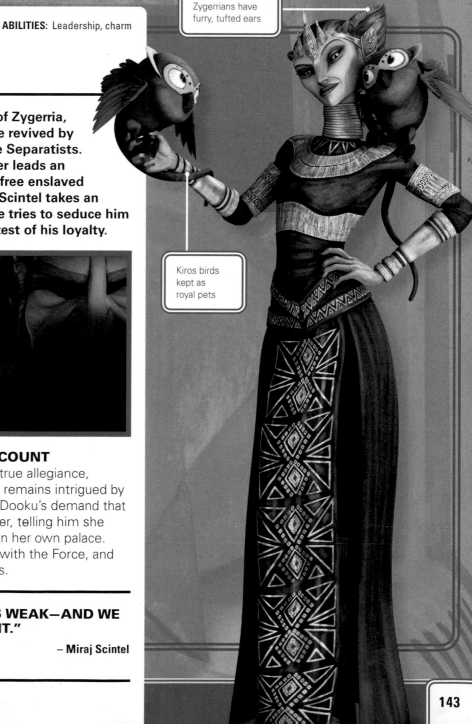

SPECIES: Zygerrian
HEIGHT: 1.85 m (6 ft 1 in)
ALLEGIANCE: Separatists
HOMEWORLD: Zygerria

ABILITIES: Leadership, charm

Zygerrians have furry, tufted ears

Kiros birds kept as royal pets

Miraj Scintel is queen of Zygerria, an ancient slave empire revived by a new alliance with the Separatists. When Anakin Skywalker leads an undercover mission to free enslaved Togruta from Zygerria, Scintel takes an interest in the Jedi. She tries to seduce him while devising a cruel test of his loyalty.

ORDERS FROM THE COUNT

After Anakin reveals his true allegiance, Scintel captures him but remains intrigued by him. She refuses Count Dooku's demand that she kill her prized prisoner, telling him she won't be ordered about in her own palace. Dooku strangles Scintel with the Force, and she dies in Anakin's arms.

"THE JEDI ORDER IS WEAK—AND WE WILL HELP BREAK IT."

– Miraj Scintel

ATAI MOLEC

SPECIES: Zygerrian
HEIGHT: 1.90 m (6 ft 3 in)
ALLEGIANCE: Zygerrians
HOMEWORLD: Zygerria

ABILITIES: Armed and unarmed combat, bureaucracy, leadership, intimidation, security

Atai Molec is Zygerria's prime minister and captain of its royal guard. He seeks to expand Zygerria's cruel slave-trading empire. When Queen Scintel refuses to kill Anakin Skywalker, Molec invites Count Dooku to speak with the rebellious monarch and doesn't intervene as Dooku strangles the queen.

DARTS D'NAR

SPECIES: Zygerrian
HEIGHT: 1.89 m (6 ft 2 in)
ALLEGIANCE: Zygerrians
HOMEWORLD: Zygerria

ABILITIES: Combat, military tactics, security, leadership

Darts D'Nar is an ambitious Zygerrian commander who works with Count Dooku to round up Togruta colonists on Kiros, then send them to Zygerria to be forced into enslavement. When the Republic invades Kiros, D'Nar is drawn into fighting Obi-Wan Kenobi, not realizing the Jedi is stalling for time so his allies can defuse bombs set by the Zygerrians.

SY SNOOTLES

SPECIES: Pa'lowick
HEIGHT: 1.65 m (5 ft 5 in)
ALLEGIANCE: Neutral
HOMEWORLD: Lowick

ABILITIES: Singing, dancing, persuasion, infiltration, spying

Sy Snootles sings and dances for audiences across the galaxy. After entertaining the Hutt Council, she frees her former lover Ziro the Hutt from prison. Ziro has no idea that Jabba the Hutt has hired Sy to find Ziro's diary. Once she locates it, she coolly shoots the unfortunate Ziro dead.

MORALO EVAL

SPECIES: Phindian
HEIGHT: 1.75 m (5 ft 9 in)
ALLEGIANCE: Neutral
HOMEWORLD: Phindar

ABILITIES: Armed and unarmed combat, leadership, technical abilities, speeder and starship piloting

Moralo Eval is the creator of the Box, a testing ground for bounty hunters. Eval and Count Dooku use the Box to select a team of hunters to kidnap Chancellor Palpatine on Naboo. Eval intends to lead this mission but is demoted to getaway driver and soon finds himself back in prison.

GARNAC

SPECIES: Trandoshan
HEIGHT: 2.1 m (6 ft 11 in)
ALLEGIANCE: Neutral
HOMEWORLD: Trandosha

ABILITIES: Armed and unarmed combat, tracking, survival, leadership, sharpshooting

Garnac is an evil Trandoshan who leads a hunting party that tracks down captured people for sport on the moon Wasskah. Ahsoka Tano and Chewbacca prove difficult prey, however. They survive the cruel hunt, outwit the hunters, and confront them aboard their ship. There, Ahsoka Force-pushes Garnac to his death.

DAR

SPECIES: Trandoshan
HEIGHT: 1.98 m (6 ft 6 in)
ALLEGIANCE: Neutral
HOMEWORLD: Trandosha

ABILITIES: Armed and unarmed combat, tracking, survival

Dar is Garnac's son, an inexperienced yet cruel young hunter eager to prove his worth on Wasskah. Dar's lack of expertise dooms him: while battling Ahsoka Tano in the moon's jungles, he is impaled on a sharp root. His father blames the Jedi for Dar's death and vows revenge.

GAMORREAN GUARD

SPECIES: Gamorrean
HEIGHT: Varies
ALLEGIANCE: Neutral
HOMEWORLD: Gamorr

ABILITIES: Armed and unarmed combat, intimidation

Gamorreans are often seen as big, dumb brutes employed as guards by the Hutts and other crime bosses. They use crude weapons and primitive tactics, but their great strength makes them intimidating. Gamorreans guard Jabba the Hutt in his palace on Tatooine.

NIKTO GUARD

SPECIES: Nikto
HEIGHT: Varies
ALLEGIANCE: Neutral
HOMEWORLD: Kintan

ABILITIES: Armed and unarmed combat, security

Several Nikto species live on Kintan. Niktos frequently hire on as mercenaries and pirates for criminal gangs, as many Niktos are effective fighters who respect power and will serve happily if promised loot, grog, and chances to make trouble. The Nikto were once enslaved by the Hutts, and many still work for them.

PINTU SON-EL

SPECIES: Moyn
HEIGHT: 1.88 m (6 ft 2 in)
ALLEGIANCE: Neutral
HOMEWORLD: Coruscant

ABILITIES: Intimidation, persuasion, negotiations

Pintu Son-El is a petty criminal who scrapes by lending credits and striking dirty deals in the lower levels of Coruscant. When Rafa Martez fails to pay back a loan as quickly as Pintu would like, he and his thugs visit her sister Trace to shake her down, but they are driven away by Trace's new friend Ahsoka Tano.

TEE VA

SPECIES: Moogan
HEIGHT: 2.31 m (7 ft 7 in)
ALLEGIANCE: Neutral
HOMEWORLD: Mooga

ABILITIES: Combat, smuggling, infiltration

Tee Va is a smuggler who sells contraband goods on Mandalore. To increase profits, he dilutes tea with high levels of slabin, causing a rash of illnesses among children. Va's arrest kicks off an investigation that leads all the way to Almec, Mandalore's prime minister, whom Duchess Satine thought was an ally.

BANNAMU

SPECIES: Patrolian
HEIGHT: 1.26 m (4 ft 2 in)
ALLEGIANCE: Neutral
HOMEWORLD: Coruscant

ABILITIES: Stealth, infiltration, stealing

Bannamu is a small-time pickpocket who slips Ahsoka Tano's lightsaber off her belt. Ahsoka is determined to retrieve her lightsaber without having to tell Anakin Skywalker of her mistake. She tracks down the thief with the help of the Jedi Master Tera Sinube.

HAL'STED

SPECIES: Siniteen
HEIGHT: 1.88 m (6 ft 2 in)
ALLEGIANCE: Neutral
HOMEWORLD: Rattatak

ABILITIES: Armed and unarmed combat, intimidation, leadership

Hal'Sted is a pirate who takes young Asajj Ventress as payment for a debt owed to him by the Nightsisters. They live on the wild frontier planet Rattatak. After Weequay bandits kill Hal'Sted, the Jedi Ky Narec takes Asajj as his Padawan, teaching her the ways of the Force.

CASSIE CRYAR

SPECIES: Terrelian Jango Jumper
HEIGHT: 1.82 m (6 ft)
ALLEGIANCE: Neutral
HOMEWORLD: Coruscant
ABILITIES: Armed and unarmed combat, agility, speed

Cassie Cryar kills a fellow criminal to gain possession of Ahsoka Tano's lost lightsaber, then flees across Coruscant when Ahsoka tracks her down. Cryar's agility helps her evade Ahsoka, but Jedi Master Sinube outthinks her, tracks her down, and brings her to justice.

IONE MARCY

SPECIES: Salenga
HEIGHT: 1.78 m (5 ft 10 in)
ALLEGIANCE: Neutral
HOMEWORLD: Coruscant
ABILITIES: Powerful friends

Ione Marcy is a small-time criminal on Coruscant who teams up with Cassie Cryar to obtain Ahsoka Tano's lightsaber. She pretends to be an innocent bystander, but Jedi Tera Sinube sees through Ione's act and plants a tracker on her. When Ione meets up with Cryar, Sinube takes both criminals into custody and retrieves Ahsoka's weapon.

GHA NACHKT

SPECIES: Trandoshan
HEIGHT: 1.75 m (5 ft 9 in)
ALLEGIANCE: Neutral
HOMEWORLD: Trandosha
ABILITIES: Starship piloting and repairs, droid programming

Gha Nachkt is a scavenger who earns credits repairing droids, weapons, and gear found in the aftermath of space battles. After the Battle of Bothawui, he spots R2-D2 floating in space and tries to sell the droid to General Grievous. When Nachkt pushes too hard for extra credits, Grievous kills him.

FONG DO

SPECIES: Nautolan
HEIGHT: 1.88 m (6 ft 2 in)
ALLEGIANCE: Neutral
HOMEWORLD: Coruscant
ABILITIES: Armed and unarmed combat, negotiations, intimidation

Fong Do is one of many small-time crooks trying to scrape by in a tough galaxy by not worrying about staying on the right side of the law. He can often be found in grubby cantinas in the underlevels of Coruscant. Fong Do confronts Ahsoka Tano and Plo Koon when the Jedi look for leads to help find hostages taken by Aurra Sing and Boba Fett.

DUCHESS SATINE KRYZE

PASSIONATE PACIFIST

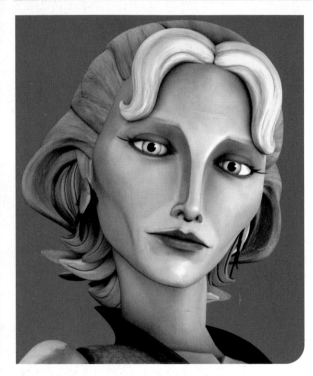

> ## "I REMEMBER A TIME WHEN JEDI WERE NOT GENERALS BUT PEACEKEEPERS."
>
> – Duchess Satine Kryze

Duchess Satine Kryze is a passionate voice for peace in the galaxy. As Mandalore's leader, she has stayed neutral in the Clone Wars. Satine rejects her homeworld's violent past and works to create a prosperous and peaceful future. It's a vision her enemies will do anything to prevent.

AN OLD BOND

Years ago, Obi-Wan Kenobi and his master Qui-Gon Jinn kept Satine safe during violent upheavals on Mandalore. The noblewoman and the Padawan fell in love. Obi-Wan would have left the Jedi Order if Satine had asked, but she did not. Both look back on their past with regret as well as relief. When Obi-Wan investigates disturbing events on Mandalore, he is reunited with Satine. The two quarrel about almost everything but discover that they still have strong feelings for each other.

The Kryze clan is far from united in support of Satine's dream of a peaceful Mandalore. Satine's sister, Bo-Katan, is a high-ranking member of

Hair styled in Kalevalan fashion

Soothing colors used on gown

Death Watch, an underground group of commandos seeking to overthrow Satine and restore Mandalore's traditions. Both Kryzes want what's best for their world but disagree completely on what that means.

FIGHT FOR THE FUTURE

Satine foils a Separatist plot to trick the Republic into invading Mandalore, outfoxes traitors close to her, and escapes several assassination attempts. But her luck runs out when Death Watch's leader, Pre Vizsla, allies himself with Maul, concocting a phony invasion in which Death Watch appear as heroes. Vizsla overthrows Satine and imprisons her. Bo-Katan frees her sister with Obi-Wan's help, but Satine's freedom is brief. As Obi-Wan watches in horror, Maul strikes the Duchess down, ending her life.

TIMELINE	
22 BSW4	Becomes leader of the Council of Neutral Systems
21 BSW4	Is betrayed by Pre Vizsla and discovers Death Watch plot against her
21 BSW4	Escapes assassination attempts on journey to Coruscant and after reaching planet
21 BSW4	Delivers holomessage to Senator Amidala that prevents Republic invasion of Mandalore
21 BSW4	Recruits Jedi Padawan Ahsoka Tano to tutor promising government cadets
21 BSW4	Sentences Prime Minister Almec to prison for treason
19 BSW4	Overthrown by Vizsla and killed by Maul

PRE VIZSLA

DEATH WATCH LEADER

As governor of Concordia, one of Mandalore's moons, Pre Vizsla helps Duchess Satine Kryze hunt down the Mandalorian commandos known as Death Watch. But Vizsla is secretly Death Watch's leader and Satine's enemy. He is determined to restore Mandalore's warrior heritage, and his obsessive quest to achieve this goal costs him his life.

RECLAIMING THE PAST

Pre Vizsla rises to power as the governor of Concordia. He appears to support Satine and her goals, but he secretly plots with Count Dooku to take over Mandalore. Their plan is to provoke a Republic invasion that will make Death Watch's commandos look like heroic resisters, inspiring Mandalorians to reject Satine's philosophy of pacifism and neutrality. When the plot fails, Vizsla angrily confronts Dooku, who scars Vizsla's face with his lightsaber.

Increasingly bitter, Vizsla vows revenge on Dooku and searches for new allies to help him achieve his dream. He seeks out Lux Bonteri, who wants to avenge the death of his mother at Dooku's hands. But on Carlac, Ahsoka Tano helps Lux realize that Vizsla has gone mad and Death Watch has become little more than a criminal gang, spreading violence and terror.

PERILOUS ALLIANCE

Vizsla later pledges allegiance to Maul, with Death Watch commandos serving as shock troops in Maul's Shadow Collective crime syndicate. Vizsla and Maul stage a phony invasion of Mandalore that Death Watch repels. Hailed as a hero, Vizsla overthrows Satine but betrays Maul, who challenges him to a duel for leadership of Death Watch. Vizsla fights well but is struck down by his former ally.

SPECIES: Human
HEIGHT: 1.83 m (6 ft)
ALLEGIANCE: Death Watch
HOMEWORLD: Mandalore

ABILITIES: Combat, excellent marksman, leadership

Traditional Mandalorian design on armor

WESTAR-35 pistols in hip holsters

TIMELINE

21 BSW4	Reveals himself as Death Watch's leader
21 BSW4	Conspires with Count Dooku to raise army on Concordia in preparation for Republic assault
21 BSW4	Sends assassin to kill Duchess Satine on Coruscant
21 BSW4	Postpones uprising after Senate votes against invading Mandalore
20 BSW4	Massacres Ming Po village on Carlac and duels Ahsoka Tano
20 BSW4	Alliance between Dooku and Death Watch ends, with Dooku scarring Vizsla
19 BSW4	Establishes Death Watch camp on Zanbar
19 BSW4	Joins Maul's Shadow Collective, stages attack on Mandalore, with Vizsla's commandos "saving" planet
19 BSW4	Ousts Satine and takes over Mandalore
19 BSW4	Killed in duel with Maul, who takes his place

ANCIENT HEIRLOOM

The Darksaber was created by the first Mandalorian to join the Jedi Order, then stolen from Coruscant by Mandalorian warriors. The black-bladed lightsaber becomes an heirloom of the Vizsla clan and a symbol of Mandalorian strength.

"THAT WOMAN TARNISHES THE VERY NAME MANDALORIAN. DEFEND HER, IF YOU WILL."

– Pre Vizsla

PRIME MINISTER ALMEC

MANDALORIAN TRAITOR

Mandalorian armor gilded to reflect rank

SPECIES: Human
HEIGHT: 1.89 m (6 ft 2 in)
ALLEGIANCE: Shadow Collective

HOMEWORLD: Mandalore
ABILITIES: Diplomacy, political skills

Prime Minister Almec pledges loyalty to Duchess Satine Kryze but secretly works to undermine her. He gains his riches by smuggling black-market goods despite the harm it does to Mandalorians. Maul frees Almec from prison and installs him as a puppet leader while ruling from the shadows. Almec, a cunning political survivor, vows to restore the warrior traditions of the Mandalorians.

A NEW CIVIL WAR

Almec's ascent sparks a new civil war on Mandalore with Bo-Katan Kryze leading former Death Watch commandos and Republic forces against Mandalorians loyal to Maul. Almec is captured by Bo-Katan and is killed by Gar Saxon to prevent him from revealing Maul's plans against the Jedi.

"MANDALORE WILL BE STRONG, AND WE WILL BE KNOWN AS THE WARRIORS WE WERE ALWAYS MEANT TO BE!"

– Prime Minister Almec

BO-KATAN KRYZE

MANDALORIAN WARRIOR

SPECIES: Human
HEIGHT: 1.8 m (5 ft 11 in)
ALLEGIANCE: Death Watch, Mandalore, Nite Owls

HOMEWORLD: Mandalore
ABILITIES: Armed and unarmed combat, aerial combat, leadership

Expert warrior Bo-Katan Kryze is a member of Death Watch dedicated to overthrowing her sister Duchess Satine Kryze. But when Maul kills Pre Vizsla and declares himself Death Watch's new leader, Bo-Katan risks her life to oppose the rule of this new regime. She leads a group of rebel commandos dedicated to removing Maul and restoring Mandalorian rule.

> **"NO OUTSIDER WILL EVER RULE MANDALORE."**
>
> – Bo-Katan Kryze

UNLIKELY ALLIES
Bo-Katan is suspicious of Death Watch's alliance with Maul, but Pre Vizsla assures her he'll betray Maul once Mandalore is theirs. Everything goes wrong as Maul kills both Satine and Vizsla, forcing Bo-Katan to do the unthinkable and seek an alliance with the Jedi and the Republic.

Bo-Katan's fighters are known as the Nite Owls

Bo-Katan is an expert shot even in aerial combat

AMIS

SPECIES: Human
HEIGHT: 1.68 m (5 ft 6 in)
ALLEGIANCE: Mandalore

HOMEWORLD: Mandalore
ABILITIES: Government studies, investigative skills

Amis is an idealistic cadet at Mandalore's Royal Academy of Government who helps uncover a smuggling ring masterminded by Prime Minister Almec. After Maul deposes Duchess Satine Kryze, Amis works with the Nite Owls—a group of Mandalorian warriors—in a brave but vain effort to rescue her.

GAR SAXON

SPECIES: Human
HEIGHT: 1.89 m (6 ft 2 in)
ALLEGIANCE: Shadow Collective

HOMEWORLD: Mandalore
ABILITIES: Commando tactics, aerial combat specialist, strategic awareness

Mandalorian super commando Gar Saxon frees Maul from a Separatist prison on Prime Minister Almec's orders, then fights for Maul's Shadow Collective. During the Siege of Mandalore, Maul abandons Saxon, who is captured by the Republic.

KORKIE KRYZE

SPECIES: Human
HEIGHT: 1.65 m (5 ft 5 in)
ALLEGIANCE: Mandalore
HOMEWORLD: Mandalore

ABILITIES: Leadership, government studies, investigative skills

The nephew of Mandalore's pacifist ruler Duchess Satine, Korkie Kryze is an able student at the Royal Academy of Government. Korkie and his fellow cadets break up a black-market operation run by Prime Minister Almec and later join the fight to save Satine from Maul's clutches.

LAGOS

SPECIES: Human
HEIGHT: 1.65 m (5 ft 5 in)
ALLEGIANCE: Mandalore
HOMEWORLD: Mandalore

ABILITIES: Government studies, investigative skills, speeder piloting

A cautious but capable student at the Royal Academy of Government, Lagos helps her fellow cadets expose Prime Minister Almec's black-market dealings. She tries to free Duchess Satine from captivity after Maul seizes Mandalore's throne.

MANDALORIAN ROYAL GUARD

SPECIES: Human
AVERAGE HEIGHT: 1.89 m (6 ft 2 in)
ALLEGIANCE: Mandalore
HOMEWORLD: Mandalore
ABILITIES: Close combat operations, ceremonial duties

The ornate helmets and polished armor worn by the Mandalorian Royal Guard recall the planet's glorious traditions. But unlike the warrior clans of old, Duchess Satine's guards are trained to show restraint when possible, in keeping with her philosophy of pacifism.

SONIEE

SPECIES: Human
HEIGHT: 1.63 m (5 ft 4 in)
ALLEGIANCE: Mandalore
HOMEWORLD: Mandalore
ABILITIES: Government studies, investigative skills, computer infiltration, data-slicing

A tech-savvy cadet at Mandalore's Royal Academy of Government, Soniee uses her slicing skills to gain access to secure warehouses, allowing the cadets to reveal Prime Minister Almec's smuggling operations. She later joins the unsuccessful effort to free Duchess Satine from Maul.

ROOK KAST

SPECIES: Human
HEIGHT: 1.7 m (5 ft 7 in)
ALLEGIANCE: Shadow Collective
HOMEWORLD: Mandalore
ABILITIES: Commando tactics, aerial combat specialist, strategic awareness

Rook Kast leads the super commandos who pledge themselves to Maul. She fights for him on Zanbar, Ord Mantell, Vizsla Keep 09, and saves Maul from death on Dathomir. During the Siege of Mandalore, Rook battles Ahsoka Tano.

URSA WREN

SPECIES: Human
HEIGHT: 1.85 m (6 ft 1 in)
ALLEGIANCE: Death Watch, Nite Owls
HOMEWORLD: Krownest
ABILITIES: Commando tactics, combat abilities, aerial combat specialist, leadership

Ursa Wren is a former member of Death Watch, who joins the Nite Owls, led by Bo-Katan Kryze. Wren then helps recruit Ahsoka Tano and fights to free Mandalore from Maul's grip, alongside clone troops.

THE FATHER

SPECIES: The Ones
HEIGHT: 2.48 m (8 ft 2 in)
ALLEGIANCE: The Force
HOMEWORLD: Mortis

ABILITIES: Force sensitivity,
leadership, persuasion, flight,
erase memories

The realm of Mortis is home
to the Ones, a trio of
powerful, mysterious Force
wielders. The Father strives
to balance the
power of his
light-side Daughter
and his dark-side Son. When
the Father senses his time
is nearing its end, he tries to
convince Anakin Skywalker
to maintain that balance
once he is gone.

THE DAUGHTER

SPECIES: The Ones
HEIGHT: 2.13 m (7 ft)
ALLEGIANCE: The Force
(light side)

HOMEWORLD: Mortis
ABILITIES: Force sensitivity,
transfer life force

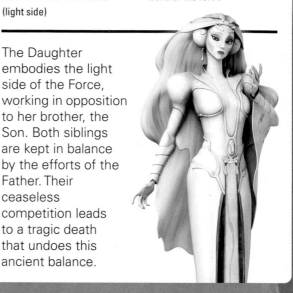

The Daughter
embodies the light
side of the Force,
working in opposition
to her brother, the
Son. Both siblings
are kept in balance
by the efforts of the
Father. Their
ceaseless
competition leads
to a tragic death
that undoes this
ancient balance.

THE SON

SPECIES: The Ones
HEIGHT: 2.2 m (7 ft 3 in)
ALLEGIANCE: The Force
(dark side)

HOMEWORLD: Mortis
ABILITIES: Force sensitivity,
persuasion, trickery,
foreknowledge

The Son embodies the dark
side of the Force and yearns
to escape Mortis. To free
himself, he plots against
the Father and the Daughter
while seeking to seduce
Anakin Skywalker by
showing him a vision of
the future he will help
bring about. This unleashes
catastrophic events for
the Ones.

MORAI

SPECIES: Convor
HEIGHT: 0.2 m (8 in)
ALLEGIANCE: The Force
(light side)

HOMEWORLD: Mortis
ABILITIES: Force sensitivity

On Mortis, the Daughter saves Ahsoka Tano
by sacrificing her own essence. But is she
entirely gone? An observer might wonder after
spotting Morai, a convor who watches over
Ahsoka and lingers in places important to her.

ORPHNE

SPECIES: Sollux
HEIGHT: 1.75 m (5 ft 9 in)
ALLEGIANCE: Neutral
HOMEWORLD: Aleen

ABILITIES: Force sensitivity, agility, riddles

Orphne is a strange being who dwells in the fairyland located below the surface of quake-ridden Aleen and commands strange magic that keeps the two realms in balance. She challenges C-3PO and R2-D2 with riddles when the droids stray into her domain while on a mercy mission to help Aleen and its inhabitants.

DARTH BANE

SPECIES: Human (Force vision)
HEIGHT: Unknown
ALLEGIANCE: Sith
HOMEWORLD: Moraband

ABILITIES: Force sensitivity, lightsaber combat, military tactics, agility, leadership, intimidation

Darth Bane rebuilt the Sith Order centuries ago, creating the Rule of Two: the Sith would consist of a master and an apprentice who'd constantly test each other while working against the Jedi in secret. For his final Force trial, Yoda confronts a vision of Bane on the ancient Sith tombworld of Moraband.

FORCE PRIESTESSES

SPECIES: Unknown
HEIGHT: 1.85 m (6 ft 1 in)
ALLEGIANCE: The Force
HOMEWORLD: Force Planet

ABILITIES: Force sensitivity, shape-shifting

These five mysterious beings dwell on a mystical world at the heart of the galaxy. They are avatars of the connections between the living Force and the cosmic Force. They take the names Serenity, Joy, Anger, Confusion, and Sadness and exhibit these emotions. The beings test Yoda during his mystical exploration of the Force.

SHMI SKYWALKER

SPECIES: Human (Force vision)
HEIGHT: 1.63 m (5 ft 4 in)
ALLEGIANCE: Neutral

HOMEWORLD: Tatooine
ABILITIES: Mechanical repairs, maintenance, survival, moisture farming

The Force is immensely powerful on Mortis, helping spawn visions of those who have died and passed into its energies. Qui-Gon Jinn is able to take form on Mortis, speaking with his former students. But such possibilities can be used to deceive: the Son tries to trick Anakin with a vision of his mother, Shmi.

WAG TOO

Tail held high for balance

SPECIES: Lurmen
HEIGHT: 1.03 m (3 ft 5 in)
ALLEGIANCE: Neutral
HOMEWORLD: Maridun

ABILITIES: Scouting, agility, healing

Wag Too is a young Lurmen healer who helps Anakin Skywalker recover from his injuries on Maridun. He is impatient with the peaceful approach of his father, Tee Watt Kaa, and fights back against Lok Durd's Separatist droids when they attack the Lurmen colony. He uses his speed and agility to help the Jedi and clones defeat the droids.

TEE WATT KAA

SPECIES: Lurmen
HEIGHT: 1.03 m (3 ft 5 in)
ALLEGIANCE: Neutral

HOMEWORLD: Maridun
ABILITIES: Leadership, persuasion, debate

Tee Watt Kaa is the founder of a Lurmen colony on Maridun and a passionate believer in the peaceful way of thinking known as Te Padka. Kaa refuses to fight even in defense, believing that war corrupts and destroys everything it touches. His beliefs are sorely tested when Lok Durd brings a Separatist army to his doorstep, forcing the peaceful colonists to make a painful choice.

Beard made stiff with apis wax

CUT LAWQUANE

Ancient blaster owned by Suu Lawquane

SPECIES: Human (clone)
HEIGHT: 1.83 m (6 ft)
ALLEGIANCE: Neutral
HOMEWORLD: Saleucami

ABILITIES: Armed and unarmed combat, military tactics, reconnaissance, farming

Cut Lawquane defied his programming early in the war and deserted the Republic, seeking a new life as a farmer on Saleucami. He finds Suu Lawquane and helps raise her two children. But the war catches up with Cut—clone troopers leave an injured Captain Rex to recuperate in his family's barn, and Separatist commando droids attack the Lawquane farm.

SUU LAWQUANE

SPECIES: Twi'lek
HEIGHT: 1.85 m (6 ft 1 in)
ALLEGIANCE: Neutral
HOMEWORLD: Saleucami

ABILITIES: Farming, armed combat

Suu Lawquane raises two children on her Saleucami farm with the help of Cut, a clone deserter. She dares to dream that the war tearing apart the galaxy will spare her family. When clones arrive on her farm with an injured Captain Rex, Suu is tempted to insist they move along. However, she can't ignore Rex's plight and allows him to rest and heal in the barn.

SHAEEAH LAWQUANE

SPECIES: Human/Twi'lek
HEIGHT: 1.15 m (3 ft 9 in)
ALLEGIANCE: Neutral
HOMEWORLD: Saleucami

ABILITIES: Farming

Shaeeah Lawquane lives a quiet life on her family's Saleucami farm with her mother Suu, her brother Jek, and her stepfather Cut. She is stunned when she finds an armored stranger, named Rex, in the family barn whose face is the same as Cut's. When Shaeeah and Jek accidentally activate Separatist droids, Cut and Rex must fight to protect them.

JEK LAWQUANE

SPECIES: Human/Twi'lek
HEIGHT: 0.95 m (3 ft 1 in)
ALLEGIANCE: Neutral
HOMEWORLD: Saleucami

ABILITIES: Farming

Jek Lawquane is a Saleucami farmboy who does his chores and draws pictures of people and places he can only imagine. The war dividing the galaxy seems to have nothing to do with him until he and his sister awaken a squad of deadly Separatist commando droids. Suddenly that distant war has grown terrifyingly close.

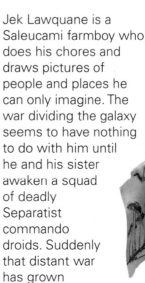

SAW GERRERA

SPECIES: Human
HEIGHT: 1.87 m (6 ft 2 in)
ALLEGIANCE: Onderon rebels
HOMEWORLD: Onderon

ABILITIES: Armed and unarmed combat, leadership, reconnaissance, infiltration

Saw Gerrera is a hot-tempered rebel, who is part of a group dedicated to freeing the planet Onderon from the Separatists. Saw wants to be the rebels' leader and feels bitter when his sister Steela is picked instead. During a battle against the Separatists, Saw shoots down an enemy gunship that crashes and kills Steela. Broken-hearted and wracked with guilt, Saw vows to keep fighting evil in all its forms.

STEELA GERRERA

Expert shot with a range of blasters

SPECIES: Human
HEIGHT: 1.79 m (5 ft 10 in)
ALLEGIANCE: Onderon rebels
HOMEWORLD: Onderon

ABILITIES: Armed and unarmed combat, leadership, reconnaissance, infiltration, sharpshooting

Steela Gerrera is an Onderon freedom fighter battling King Rash and his Separatist allies. She sees herself as more soldier than leader, leaving the fiery speeches to her brother Saw. But Steela comes to realize that she's a far better leader than Saw. She assumes command of the Onderon rebels but is killed in the climactic battle for her homeworld.

GENERAL TANDIN

SPECIES: Human
HEIGHT: 1.77 m (5 ft 10 in)
ALLEGIANCE: Neutral
HOMEWORLD: Onderon

ABILITIES: Armed and unarmed combat, military tactics, security, leadership

Akenathen Tandin is a general in Onderon's royal militia. After Sanjay Rash overthrows Onderon's King Dendup, Tandin at first serves the new regime, fearing that a civil war would only cause more suffering. But Saw Gerrera convinces Tandin he was wrong. The general helps save Dendup from execution and joins the fight against Rash and the Separatists.

KING DENDUP

SPECIES: Human
HEIGHT: 1.68 m (5 ft 6 in)
ALLEGIANCE: Neutral
HOMEWORLD: Onderon

ABILITIES: Leadership, persuasion

King Ramsis Dendup rules Onderon and insists on staying neutral in the Clone War, seeing both the Republic and the Confederacy of Independent Systems as corrupt regimes. He is overthrown by Sanjay Rash, who imprisons him and allies Onderon with the Separatists. Onderon's rebels save Dendup from execution and restore him to the throne.

LAMA SU

SPECIES: Kaminoan
HEIGHT: 2.29 m (7 ft 6 in)
ALLEGIANCE: Kaminoans
HOMEWORLD: Kamino

ABILITIES: Leadership, genetic engineering, legislative strategy, negotiating, persuasion

Lama Su is Kamino's prime minister and oversees the creation of the Republic clone army. This project brings his planet great wealth but also puts it in danger as a Separatist military target. Su is secretly loyal to the Sith, and he works to prevent the Republic from learning about the clone army's origins, inhibitor chips, and ultimate purpose.

NALA SE

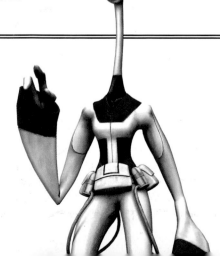

SPECIES: Kaminoan
HEIGHT: 2.13 m (7 ft)
ALLEGIANCE: Kaminoans
HOMEWORLD: Kamino

ABILITIES: Genetic engineering, medical science, patient care, keeping secrets

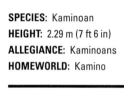

Nala Se is Kamino's chief medical scientist. She genuinely cares for the clones, risking her life to treat their injuries, but also argues that they are Kaminoan property. After Tup's inhibitor chip malfunctions, Se warns Lama Su and the Sith what has happened. Se also tries to stop the Jedi and the Republic from investigating the chips and discovering their sinister purpose.

CHAM SYNDULLA

SPECIES: Twi'lek
HEIGHT: 1.9 m (6 ft 3 in)
ALLEGIANCE: Free Ryloth Movement
HOMEWORLD: Ryloth

ABILITIES: Armed and unarmed combat, infiltration, reconnaissance, survival, leadership, animal handling

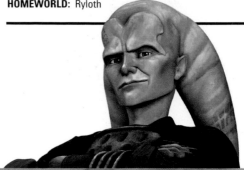

Cham Syndulla is a freedom fighter on Ryloth. He leads the resistance against Wat Tambor's Separatist army but distrusts the Republic, seeing Ryloth's Senator Orn Free Taa as a hopelessly corrupt politician. After Jedi Master Mace Windu brokers a truce between the two, Syndulla joins forces with the Republic and plays a crucial role in freeing the planet.

GOBI GLIE

Shirt in need of a wash

SPECIES: Twi'lek
HEIGHT: 1.84 m (6 ft)
ALLEGIANCE: Free Ryloth Movement
HOMEWORLD: Ryloth
ABILITIES: Combat, reconnaissance, survival, music

Gobi Glie is a member of the Free Ryloth Movement and battles alongside Cham Syndulla against the droid armies occupying Ryloth. He and his fellow fighters survive the initial Separatist assault when Jedi General Ima-Gun Di gives his life so they can escape. This is a sacrifice Glie vows to remember. In addition to his skills as a guerilla, Glie is a talented musician and balladeer.

NUMA

SPECIES: Twi'lek
HEIGHT: 1 m (3 ft 3 in)
ALLEGIANCE: Neutral
HOMEWORLD: Ryloth

ABILITIES: Survival, local knowledge

When Separatist droids invade her hometown of Nabat on Ryloth, Numa hides in tunnels beneath the ruins. She thinks the clone troopers Boil and Waxer are also droids and is surprised when they remove their helmets to reveal human faces. Numa shows them secret paths beneath Nabat that help the Republic stop a Separatist advance.

KRISMO SODI

Electro-swords can withstand a lightsaber blade

SPECIES: Kage
HEIGHT: 1.89 m (6 ft 2 in)
ALLEGIANCE: Neutral
HOMEWORLD: Quarzite

ABILITIES: Armed and unarmed combat, martial arts, agility, milodon handling, leadership, military tactics

Krismo Sodi leads Quarzite's Kage warriors and is an agile, deadly opponent in battle. He heads up a raid on a subtram to retrieve his kidnapped sister Pluma. The vehicle is defended by Boba Fett's team of bounty hunters, who have no idea Pluma is inside of the chest they are protecting. After the Kage warriors defeat most of Fett's hunters, Krismo duels Ventress.

PLUMA SODI

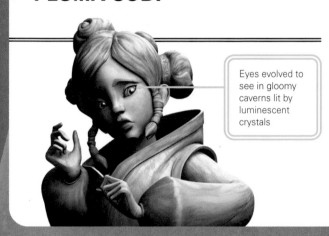

Eyes evolved to see in gloomy caverns lit by luminescent crystals

SPECIES: Kage
HEIGHT: 1.6 m (5 ft 3 in)
ALLEGIANCE: Neutral
HOMEWORLD: Quarzite

ABILITIES: Bravery, family ties

Pluma Sodi is the sister of the Kage warrior Krismo Sodi. She is kidnapped by the tyrant Otua Blank and sent to his palace aboard a subtram. To save her, Krismo battles bounty hunters hired by Blank. Asajj Ventress defeats Krismo but frees both Sodis after learning about Blank's plans.

OTUA BLANK

SPECIES: Belugan
HEIGHT: 1.98 m (6 ft 6 in)
ALLEGIANCE: Neutral
HOMEWORLD: Quarzite

ABILITIES: Leadership, persuasion, intimidation

Otua Blank is the greedy Belugan ruler of Quarzite, where his regime is opposed by bands of Kage warriors. Blank hires bounty hunters led by Boba Fett to guard a subtram carrying a kidnapped Kage, Pluma, whom he plans to marry against her will. Asajj Ventress returns Pluma to her brother when she learns of this, delivering a bound and gagged Fett instead.

KING KATUUNKO

SPECIES: Toydarian
HEIGHT: 1.52 m (5 ft)
ALLEGIANCE: Toydarians
HOMEWORLD: Toydaria

ABILITIES: Combat, leadership, negotiations

Katuunko is Toydaria's king and is determined to keep his people safe. After watching Yoda in action, he agrees to allow the Republic to establish a base on Toydaria, a decision Count Dooku vows he'll regret. Dooku sends Savage Opress to kidnap the king, but Savage murders him instead.

QIN YAZAL

SPECIES: Poletec
HEIGHT: 2.6 m (8 ft 6 in)
ALLEGIANCE: Poletec
HOMEWORLD: Skako Minor

ABILITIES: Armed and unarmed combat, military tactics, leadership, keeradak handling

Qin Yazal leads a Polotec village on Skako Minor. He accuses Anakin Skywalker and the Bad Batch of bringing war to his people but relents after he learns they are trying to free a captive clone trooper. The Republic troops then help Yazal fight Techno Union droids.

THI-SEN

SPECIES: Talz
HEIGHT: 2.48 m (8 ft 2 in)
ALLEGIANCE: Talz
HOMEWORLD: Orto Plutonia

ABILITIES: Combat, leadership, diplomacy, military tactics, narglatch riding, reconnaissance

Thi-Sen is a Talz chieftain living on Orto Plutonia who just wants peace for his people. Pantora's Chi Cho insists on fighting, so Thi-Sen does what he must. After a fierce fight kills Cho, Thi-Sen accepts Pantoran Riyo Chuchi's wise offer of peace.

THE BIG HAY-ZU

SPECIES: Patitite
HEIGHT: 0.43 m (1 ft 5 in)
ALLEGIANCE: Neutral

HOMEWORLD: Patitite Pattuna
ABILITIES: Combat, leadership, persuasion

Hay-Zu is a small tyrant with a huge ego who sends Patitite children to fight his wars. He demands that C-3PO and R2-D2 leave his planet, waving away C-3PO's request for help fixing their ship. An accident topples R2-D2 onto the king, flattening him and ending his terrible rule.

GOVERNOR ROSHTI

SPECIES: Togruta
HEIGHT: 1.98 m (6 ft 6 in)
ALLEGIANCE: Neutral
HOMEWORLD: Kiros

ABILITIES: Leadership, diplomacy, art

Governor Gupat Roshti is determined to keep Kiros' Togruta colony neutral in the Clone Wars. However, Count Dooku invades Roshti's planet and hands his people over to the Zygerrians, who enslave them. After Jedi and clones free the Togruta from the Zygerrians, Roshti vows to join the Republic.

KINDALO

SPECIES: Kindalo
HEIGHT: Varies
ALLEGIANCE: Neutral
HOMEWORLD: Aleen

ABILITIES: Create groundquakes, collective decision-making

The Kindalo are treelike beings who live in the underground caverns on Aleen. The surface's air poisons the Kindalo, forcing them to cause groundquakes to seal off their realm. C-3PO and R2-D2 encounter the Kindalo and close the breach that has put them in danger.

CASISS MIDAGATIS

SPECIES: Felucian
HEIGHT: 1.35 m (4 ft 5 in)
ALLEGIANCE: Neutral
HOMEWORLD: Felucia

ABILITIES: Farming, leadership

Casiss is the leader of Akira, a village on Felucia. He hires bounty hunter Sugi's mercenary crew to defend Akira and its nysillim crop from Hondo Ohnaka's pirates. Casiss also convinces his hired guns to work with a stranded team of Jedi. This unusual partnership succeeds, saving Casiss' people.

KING MANCHUCHO

SPECIES: Aleena
HEIGHT: 0.78 m (2 ft 7 in)
ALLEGIANCE: Republic
HOMEWORLD: Aleen

ABILITIES: Leadership, diplomacy, persuasion

Manchucho is the king of Aleen and welcomes Jedi Plo Koon's clone forces to his planet after it is devastated by groundquakes. With C-3PO serving as translator, he asks the Republic to send aid to the Aleena. The king knows of Aleen's underground inhabitants and seeks to live in peace with them.

RAFA MARTEZ

CORUSCANT SURVIVOR

Hair cut in fashion popular in underlevels

Coat stolen from careless customer at laundry

SPECIES: Human
HEIGHT: 1.68 m (5 ft 6 in)
ALLEGIANCE: Neutral
HOMEWORLD: Coruscant

ABILITIES: Armed and unarmed combat, negotiations, deal-making, repairs, laundry

Rafa Martez owns a repair hangar and a laundry in Coruscant's dangerous lower levels, but both businesses are fronts: she makes her living by doing illegal jobs for clients who don't ask too many questions. Rafa is devoted to her younger sister Trace, whom she's raised since their parents died. Rafa has tried to teach the kind-hearted Trace to beware of anyone who isn't family.

"SHE'S NOT FAMILY, TRACE. REMEMBER THAT."

– Rafa Martez

DANGEROUS SCHEME

Rafa tries to change the siblings' fortunes by agreeing to run spice for the Pyke Syndicate. She is forced to bring Trace into her scheme when the pilot she contracted backs out of the deal. Rafa soon finds she's in over her head trying to negotiate with the ruthless Pykes and their hired thugs.

TRACE MARTEZ

PILOT WITH BIG DREAMS

SPECIES: Human
HEIGHT: 1.66 m (5 ft 5 in)
ALLEGIANCE: Neutral
HOMEWORLD: Coruscant

ABILITIES: Starship piloting, armed and unarmed combat, repairs

Trace Martez dreams of escaping the depths of Coruscant and seeing the galaxy in her ship, the *Silver Angel*. Despite her sister Rafa's warnings not to trust outsiders, she instinctively helps Ahsoka Tano when the former Jedi crashes into her repair shop. But Trace's instincts to do the right thing lead her into trouble on a mission to Kessel.

ESCAPING THE PAST

When Trace discovers Rafa has filled the *Silver Angel* with spice, she impulsively drops the cargo for fear of losing her ship. But this causes bigger problems for the sisters, who now owe a massive debt to some of the most ruthless gangsters in the galactic underworld.

"I'VE GOT ONE OF THE FASTEST SHIPS AROUND."

– Trace Martez

Jacket protects against chill of the underlevels

Multitool used for repairing machinery

MORLEY

SPECIES: Anacondan
LENGTH: 4.7 m (15 ft 5 in)
ALLEGIANCE: None
HOMEWORLD: Lotho Minor

ABILITIES: Scavenging, survival, guile

A serpentine Anacondan, Morley dwells on Lotho Minor amid its trash heaps. He tricks visitors into fatal encounters with the insane Maul and then dines on their remains. Morley meets his end when he tries the same trick on Savage Opress, who strangles him.

LOTHO MINOR JUNKERS

SPECIES: Varies
HEIGHT: Varies
ALLEGIANCE: None
HOMEWORLD: Lotho Minor

ABILITIES: Survival, repairs, scavenging, unarmed combat,

Lotho Minor's junkers are a strange band of beings whose bodies consist of organic flesh as well as cybernetic parts. Their origins are mysterious, and brave scientists investigating this matter have vanished before reporting back.

AMIT NOLOFF

SPECIES: Quarren
HEIGHT: 1.82 m (6 ft)
ALLEGIANCE: None

HOMEWORLD: Iego
ABILITIES: Starship piloting, business negotiations

Amit Noloff was once a successful spice dealer, but he became trapped on Iego and went mad. Noloff tells everyone that the system is cursed by the mysterious Drol, jabbing his finger at the skies to emphasize his grim warning.

ANGELS OF IEGO

SPECIES: Angels of Iego
HEIGHT: 2.35 m (7 ft 9 in)
ALLEGIANCE: None
HOMEWORLD: Millius Prime

ABILITIES: Flight

The Angels of Iego are rumored to be the most beautiful beings in the galaxy but are believed to be simply legend. However, there is truth behind the story: the Angels lived on the moon Millius Prime until their home was stolen from them by Separatist invaders.

JAYBO HOOD

SPECIES: Human
HEIGHT: 1.4 m (4 ft 7 in)
ALLEGIANCE: None
HOMEWORLD: Iego

ABILITIES: Droid repair, tinkering, data-slicing, droid programming

Jaybo Hood lives like a king on Iego, waited on by reprogrammed battle droids. He believes in the Curse of Drol but agrees to help Anakin Skywalker and Obi-Wan Kenobi try and escape Iego. With help from Jaybo's reprogrammed vulture droids, the Jedi destroy the laser net behind the "curse."

CHIEFTAIN PIETER

SPECIES: Human
HEIGHT: 1.72 m (5 ft 8 in)
ALLEGIANCE: Ming Po

HOMEWORLD: Carlac
ABILITIES: Leadership

Pieter is the chieftain of a Ming Po community on the snowy, beautiful planet Carlac. He tries to keep the peace when Death Watch establishes a base near his town, but the raiders kidnap people and force them into servitude. Pieter demands that Death Watch return the captives and leave, but his brave stand leads to tragic results for the people he tries to protect.

TRYLA

SPECIES: Human
HEIGHT: 1.7 m (5 ft 7 in)
ALLEGIANCE: Ming Po

HOMEWORLD: Carlac
ABILITIES: Survival, patience

Tryla is Chieftain Pieter's granddaughter and one of the Ming Po captured by Death Watch and forced to serve the invaders. Pre Vizsla, Death Watch's leader, frees Tryla as Pieter demands. However, this seemingly decent act is a cruel ruse: Vizsla kills the innocent girl, and his raiders burn the town.

BATTLE DROID 513

MODEL: Custom droid
HEIGHT: 3.39 m (11 ft 1 in)
ALLEGIANCE: None
HOMEWORLD: Custom

ABILITIES: Unarmed combat, military tactics, leadership

Death Watch assembled battle droid 513 from spare parts and used it as target practice while on Carlac. After R2-D2 repairs 513, it agrees to lead a droid uprising against its cruel Death Watch masters.

LETTA TURMOND

SPECIES: Human
HEIGHT: 1.8 m (5 ft 11 in)
ALLEGIANCE: Neutral
HOMEWORLD: Coruscant

ABILITIES: Sabotage, activism

Letta Turmond believes the Jedi have become warmongers and takes a radical step to stop them: she feeds her husband nano-droids, turning him into a living bomb that rips through the Jedi Temple. She is arrested but killed in jail by Barriss Offee, who manipulated Turmond into committing the atrocious Temple bombing.

KINASH LOCK

SPECIES: Twi'lek
HEIGHT: 1.9 m (6 ft 3 in)
ALLEGIANCE: Neutral
HOMEWORLD: Kessel

ABILITIES: Bureaucracy, smuggling, persuasion, negotiations

Kinash Lock serves Kessel's King Yaruba as majordomo and supervises trade, which gives him the chance to strike deals with smugglers in the king's name. Lock hires the Martez sisters, a pair of new smugglers, to deliver spice to Oba Diah and the Pykes, a dangerous assignment demanding experience they both lack.

QUEEN JULIA

SPECIES: Bardottan
HEIGHT: 2.3 m (7 ft 7 in)
ALLEGIANCE: Neutral
HOMEWORLD: Bardotta

ABILITIES: Leadership, diplomacy

Queen Julia rules Bardotta, which is threatened by an ancient prophecy. She appeals to her old friend Jar Jar Binks for help, and he arrives with Jedi Master Mace Windu. When cultists kidnap Julia and Windu, Jar Jar tracks them to Zardossa Stix and foils the group's plan to sacrifice the queen.

FRANGAWL CULT

SPECIES: Bardottan
HEIGHT: Varies
ALLEGIANCE: Malmourral
HOMEWORLD: Bardotta

ABILITIES: Armed and unarmed combat, infiltration, kidnapping, sorcery

The Frangawl Cult ruled the planet Bardotta in its early history and worships Malmourral, the Bardottan god of death. The group begins kidnapping Dagoyan Masters to bring about an ancient prophecy, leading Queen Julia to appeal to Jar Jar Binks for assistance.

MAHTEE DUNN

SPECIES: Rodian
HEIGHT: 1.7 m (5 ft 7 in)
ALLEGIANCE: Neutral
HOMEWORLD: Rodia

ABILITIES: Maternal instinct

Mahtee Dunn is the mother of a gifted child: her son Wee has been levitating his toys since he was a baby. She is sad when a man she thinks is a Jedi comes to take Wee. Mahtee is horrified when she later learns her visitor isn't a Jedi but a bounty hunter named Cad Bane and is relieved to be reunited with Wee by real Jedi.

ROO-ROO PAGE

SPECIES: Gungan
HEIGHT: 0.49 m (1 ft 7 in)
ALLEGIANCE: Neutral
HOMEWORLD: Naboo

ABILITIES: Force sensitivity

Roo-Roo Page is a Force-sensitive girl targeted by bounty hunter Cad Bane, who is collecting potential Jedi for the evil Darth Sidious. Anakin Skywalker sets a trap for the hunter, then travels with Ahsoka Tano to rescue Roo-Roo and other children taken by Bane.

PREIGO

SPECIES: Dug
HEIGHT: 1 m (3 ft 3 in)
ALLEGIANCE: Neutral
HOMEWORLD: Malastare

ABILITIES: Leadership, negotiations, showmanship

Preigo is a Dug showman who manages a traveling circus that employs acrobats, clowns, and strange beasts. On the way to Hondo Ohnaka's pirate base on Florrum, Preigo meets five acrobats. Valuing their artistry, Priego hires the group, not realizing they are actually Jedi younglings on a mission to rescue Ahsoka Tano.

MORLIMUR SNUGG

SPECIES: Snivvian
HEIGHT: 1.88 m (6 ft 2 in)
ALLEGIANCE: Neutral
HOMEWORLD: Cybloc XII

ABILITIES: Bureaucracy, logistics

Morlimur Snugg is a no-nonsense Snivvian superintendent who keeps order aboard the Banking Clan's Cybloc Transfer Station. After two lightsaber-wielding Zabraks steal a fortune in credits and Snugg's ship, he meets with Jedi Adi Gallia and Obi-Wan Kenobi, who are on the culprits' trail.

DARTH VADER

JEDI IN DARKNESS

Helmet is integral part of life-support system

SPECIES: Human
HEIGHT: 2.03 m (6 ft 8 in)
ALLEGIANCE: Sith
HOMEWORLD: Tatooine

ABILITIES: Force sensitivity, lightsaber combat, dark-side powers, agility, leadership, intimidation

When Jedi Knight Anakin Skywalker falls to the dark side, he pledges himself to the Sith, assuming the name Darth Vader. He is then tasked with wiping out the Jedi on Coruscant and the surviving Separatist leaders on Mustafar. After destroying this opposition, Vader is nearly killed dueling Obi-Wan Kenobi and forced to don black armor to preserve his life. As far as the galaxy knows, Anakin died at the end of the Clone Wars. Vader is known as the Emperor's fearsome enforcer, and his origins are cloaked in secrecy.

"NO! NO! I WILL DO SUCH TERRIBLE THINGS..."
– Anakin Skywalker

GHOSTS OF THE PAST
Vader ponders a curious puzzle: someone has turned a Republic warship's wreckage into a memorial for fallen clones, and a familiar lightsaber lies abandoned in the snow. The man who was once Anakin Skywalker stands in silence, surrounded by memories of his former Padawan and echoes in the Force.

STORMTROOPER

SPECIES: Human
HEIGHT: Varies
ALLEGIANCE: Galactic Empire
HOMEWORLD: Varies

ABILITIES: Combat, military tactics, reconnaissance, security

When the Republic becomes the Empire, it remains a massive war machine with Star Destroyers and armies as symbols of Emperor Palpatine's might. Over time, clone troopers give way to stormtroopers, who aren't clones but recruits. While these new soldiers may lack inhibitor chips, indoctrination makes them as obedient as their clone predecessors.

SNOWTROOPER

SPECIES: Human
HEIGHT: Varies
ALLEGIANCE: Galactic Empire
HOMEWORLD: Varies

ABILITIES: Combat, military tactics, reconnaissance, survival

Like clone troopers, stormtroopers are trained for specialized roles and are given unique gear optimized for a variety of environments. Imperial snowtroopers depend on breathing hoods, insulated body gloves, and suit systems to keep warm. The Imperial squad accompanying Vader to the *Tribunal*'s crash-site includes snowtroopers.

IMPERIAL PROBE DROID

MODEL: Viper probe droid
HEIGHT: 1.6 m (5 ft 3 in)
ALLEGIANCE: Galactic Empire
MANUFACTURER: Arakyd Industries

ABILITIES: Reconnaissance, infiltration, sensor suite, blaster cannon, self-destruct

Imperial probe droids perform a range of missions, from searching planets for signs of pirates and criminals to conducting sensor scans of areas the Empire wants to investigate. They use their sensors to probe wreckage and map terrain. Probe droids are equipped with powerful transceivers, which are used to beam their discoveries to Star Destroyers and intelligence outposts for further analysis.

INDEX

Penguin Random House

Project Editors Matt Jones, Pamela Afram
Project Art Editors Jon Hall, Stefan Georgiou
Editor Vicky Armstrong
Production Editor Siu Yin Chan
Senior Producer Louise Minihane
Managing Editor Sarah Harland
Managing Art Editor Vicky Short
Publishing Director Mark Searle

For Lucasfilm
Senior Editor Brett Rector
Creative Director of Publishing Michael Siglain
Art Director Troy Alders
Story Group Leland Chee, Emily Shkoukani
Creative Art Manager Phil Szostak
Asset Management Shahana Alam, Chris Argyropoulos,
Nicole LaCoursiere, Gabrielle Levenson, Sarah Williams

DK would like to thank:
Chelsea Alon at Disney Publishing; Ruth Amos
and Laura Palosuo for editorial assistance; Nicole
Reynolds for the index; Kathryn Hill for proofreading;
Megan Douglass for Americanization; and David
McDonald for design assistance.

First American Edition, 2021
Published in the United States by DK Publishing
1450 Broadway, Suite 801, New York, NY 10018

Page design copyright © 2021 Dorling Kindersley Limited
DK, a Division of Penguin Random House LLC
21 22 23 24 25 10 9 8 7 6 5 4 3 2 1
001-323366-April/2021

Published in Great Britain by Dorling Kindersley Limited

A catalog record for this book is available from the Library of
Congress.

ISBN: 978-0-7440-3715-9

DK books are available at special discounts when purchased in
bulk for sales promotions, premiums, fundraising, or educational
use. For details, contact: DK Publishing Special Markets,
1450 Broadway, Suite 801, New York, NY 10018
SpecialSales@dk.com

Printed and bound in China

For the curious
www.dk.com

www.starwars.com

MIX
Paper from
responsible sources
FSC™ C018179

This book is made from
Forest Stewardship Council™
certified paper—one small
step in DK's commitment
to a sustainable future.